IF YOU WANT TO PREACH

IF YOU WANT TO PREACH

by
DON DE WELT

Author of *Sacred History and
Geography* and *Acts Made Actual*

In grateful acknowledgment
of those students of homiletics
who have a part in me,
and I a part in them.

PREFACE

If you *want* to preach the Word, this is the book for you.

We have two basic purposes in placing this book in your hands. First, to help you in preparing your heart for preaching. Secondly, to assist in preparing your mind for preaching.

Before and above everything else there must be the holy, honest desire on your part to be a minister of the gospel. With this desire burning in your soul you must set about so to prepare your personal devotional life that Christ may dwell in you. Only when this is true can you hope to communicate Him to others.

While the above statement is true, I am sure we all know men who are sincere Christians and have a real desire to be a preacher of the gospel and yet are unable to make themselves understood in an intelligent manner, and are hence hindered from being used of God.

We feel that it is of utmost importance to be able to preach in a logical, forceful manner. This, then, is the two-fold purpose of this book:

(1) To prepare the man.

(2) To help the prepared man to prepare the sermon.

There is in this book an attempt to enlist your personal participation. You will note in each assignment that there is something for you to do at home and in the class room.

There are new approaches to an old subject in the pages of this work. Whereas the approaches are new, they have been tested in the laboratory of the class room and pulpit for more than a decade.

We believe this book will truly help in the devotion and logic necessary to be an effective preacher of the Word of God.

CONTENTS

INTRODUCTION

This book is intended to be practical — first, last, and always. For this reason it is set up in the form of a workbook as well as a text. This material is intentionally prepared to be very personal. This being so, it should be approached in the spirit of prayer. It is the practice of our class to spend the first fifteen or twenty minutes in prayer so as to prepare our hearts for spiritual participation in the session.

Here is the first chapter with its assignments. (Each assignment is intended to be a day's work for the class.) May our Father bless your every effort as you approach this tremendous subject.

Chapter 1

The Minister of the Word as the Man of God

STIR ME

Stir me, O stir me, Lord! I care not how,
  But stir my heart in passion for the world;
Stir me to give, to go, but most to pray;
  Stir, till the blood-red banner be unfurled
O'er lands that still in heathen darkness lie,
O'er desert where no cross is lifted high.

Stir me, O stir me, Lord! till all my heart
  Is filled with strong compassion for these souls;
Till thy compelling "must" drive me to prayer;
  Till thy constraining love reach to the poles,
Far north and south, in burning, deep desire;
Till east and west are caught in love's great fire.

Stir me, O stir me, Lord! Thy heart was stirred
  By love's intensest fire, till thou didst give
Thine only Son, thy best-beloved One,
  E'en to the dreadful cross, that I might live;
Stir me to give myself so back to thee
That thou canst give thyself again through me.

—BESSIE PORTER HEAD

THE MINISTER OF THE WORD AS THE MAN OF GOD

Assignment One

Prepare a five minute speech on one of the following subjects:
1. Why I accepted Christ as my personal Saviour.
2. Why I entered the ministry.
3. Why I hate sin.
4. Why I love righteousness.
5. Why I want to go to heaven.

Suggestions:

a. Opportunity should be given for *all* members of class to speak on one of these topics.

b. A general discussion and prayer service could *follow* each class session.

c. Give *definite* reasons in your development of the subject.

Example: *Why I accepted Christ*

I accepted Christ as my personal Saviour because:
1. I *needed* a Saviour.
2. I wanted a purpose for living.
3. I saw in Him the only source of truth.

d. If you can not be personal in your development, your recitation (or speech) will not be acceptable. Make your acceptance of Christ, your discussion of the ministry, sin, righteousness, heaven, *a personal matter, a personal matter, a personal matter.*

e. In this recitation forget about your appearance, your vocabulary (or lack of it), or any of the other formal needs of a speaker. We want only to edify one another and permit the teacher to observe the native abilities of each student.

f. Give this speech everything you have by way of personal testimony.

15

Assignment Two

Take this "heart probe" for your own personal spiritual help.

Suggestions:

a. This should be done at home, preceded by prayer.

b. A discussion of these questions, based upon the answers given, could be had in class.

c. The teacher may select the questions he feels the most helpful and discuss them.

Answer these questions *Yes* or *No* and then estimate the percentage of your *Yes* or *No* (100%; 90%; 80%; 50%; 10% etc.).

1. Do I honestly feel the greatness of this mission?
Yes?———— No?———— Percentage?————————

2. If I were to receive in tomorrow's mail an opportunity to take a job that would pay me $100.00 per day, would I postpone my preparation for the ministry to make this money?
Yes?———— No?———— Why? ————————————
————————————————————— Percentage? ————

3. Do I really feel the awfulness of the loss of one soul?
Yes?———— No?———— Percentage?————————

4. Do I really believe in the value of one soul as given by Christ in Matthew 16:26?
Yes?———— No?———— Percentage?————————

5. Am I willing to lose personal possessions that one soul could be saved? For example, would I be willing to sell my car and buy food that I might stay in school?
Yes?———— No?———— Percentage?————————

6. Honestly now, could I say with Paul: "I could wish that I, myself, were anathema from Christ for my brethren's sake?" Wait a moment before answering — do not lie; let your conscience bear witness in the presence of the Holy Spirit.
Yes?———— No?———— Percentage?————————

7. Am I really conscious of the all-seeing eye of God? Do I now feel that our loving Lord is looking over my shoulder as I read these words? Is the verse of this song real to me?

All along on the road
To the soul's true abode
There's an eye watching you.
Every step that you take
This great eye is awake,
There's an eye watching you.

Yes?———— No?———— Percentage?————

8. Is there a tender yearning within for souls without? Does the love of Christ constrain me?

Yes?———— No?———— Percentage?————

9. Do I take the intensity of feelings for souls from the example of others or do I allow Christ to be my example in this?

Yes?———— No?———— Percentage?————

10. Am I more than professionally concerned over the precious immortal spirits of men?

Yes?———— No?———— Percentage?————

(Come now, my soul, no hedging in your answer.)

11. With a full knowledge of the meaning and application of James 3:1 (read it), am I willing to enter the ministry?

Yes?———— No?———— Percentage?————

12. If I am made responsible for one thousand souls during my lifetime as a preacher, responsible for their spiritual nurture, for their eternal destiny, am I yet willing to set my hand and heart to this task?

Yes?———— No?———— Percentage?————

13. What is my present attitude toward my learning? Am I going to be perfectly willing to receive all that is taught without personal investigation of the Word of God to see if these things are so? (Acts 17:11).

Yes?———— No?———— Percentage?————

14. When I know that all men are fallible, am I yet going to act like I believe some are infallible? In other words, am I too intellectually lazy to study for myself?

Yes?———— No?———— Percentage?————

15. Who are the blind that follow the blind in the work of religion?

Your answer ————————————————

16. Can I agree and not be arrogant and disagree and not be disagreeable?

Yes?———— No?———— Percentage?————

Read I Cor. 13:4-7.

17. As I spend time studying the Bible, am I growing in the likeness of the Saviour? (In this connection, ask yourself the question: For whom am I studying God's word? Is it for others first or for myself? Read Romans 2:1-3 and make personal application.)

Yes?———— No?———— Percentage?————

18. Will I conscientiously try to please God in my preparation and delivery of messages? Remember, the message is not prepared to please this brother or that brother, but God, our Heavenly Father.

Yes?———— No?———— Percentage?————

Can this be done without conscious effort on your part?

If so, how? ————————————————

19. Can I honestly say that I feel that I have a divine message to communicate?

Yes?———— No?———— Percentage?————

20. Does the fact that we have to couch the message in our own words hinder the feeling that it is a divine message?

Yes?———— No?———— Why? ————————

21. Do I really believe the Bible, or only the parts I can grasp rationally? Which? ————————————————

22. What does Paul mean by saying that the Word is the "sword of the Spirit"? (Eph. 6:17).

Answer ————————————————————

23. Is there any power present in my preaching other than the truth?

Yes?———— No?———— If so, what is it?————

24. What would one soul saved through my ministry mean to me? What would be the first thought of my heart?

Honestly check one:

———— a. The acclaim in the congratulations of men.

———— b. The feeling of personal accomplishment.

—— c. The record of it in a brotherhood paper.
—— d. The joy in heaven on the part of God and the holy
       angels.

Be honest, O my soul. Do not even now play once again the hypocrite in your answer. Let the Spirit of God elevate your joys to a higher plane.

Assignment Three

Read the following discussion of the subject.
Suggestions:
   a. Do this at home.
   b. Think of your personal relationship to the subject as discovered in the "heart probe."
   c. After reading it carefully, answer from memory the questions which follow.
   d. The teacher could discuss in class some of your answers or some of the questions he deemed the most important.

The Scriptures tell us: that David, the shepherd boy, was able to face the giant of the Philistines unafraid; that Moses stood before all the might of the kingdom of Egypt with a courage that gave him victory; that Elijah challenged the priests of Baal single handed at the contest of Mount Carmel. Preacher friend, there was one characteristic that made these acts of courage possible; the same characteristic that Paul employed when referring to Timothy. He said: "But thou, *O man of God* . . ." (I Tim. 6:11). David was the slayer of Goliath, Moses the mighty deliverer of God's children, Elijah victor at Carmel's contest, *only because they knew and realized they were God's men.* They knew God had called them to the task; that God would provide the strength and wisdom to overcome any and all obstacles. In a very real sense, they knew God was with them and they were His men.

Something of this same holy conviction must be the portion of every evangelist of the gospel today. Every minister should stand before the congregation in full realization of the designation given him by the Holy Spirit..."*Thou, O man of God.*" We are God's men in a very real sense. The task we accomplish is not ours, but His. The results of our ministry are not ours, but His.

What should we then, as men of God, know and realize con-cerning our task of preaching the Word?

1. We should know and realize something of *the greatness of this task.*

The greatest position in all the earth is that of preaching the message of God.

You occupy, as a minister of the Word, a greater position than the president of our country. Into the hands of the president falls the responsibility of deciding upon great and important issues. He makes decisions that affect the nation and the world. But, into your hands falls even a greater responsibility, the awful and eternal responsibility of the destiny of the human spirit, both for time and eternity. To you is given the task of providing for man's hope, happiness and eternal life. Think of it and prepare to preach accordingly.

The greatest obligations in the universe are yours.

The words of Paul to that young preacher of long ago still apply with mighty force today: "I charge thee *in the sight of God.*" As ministers of the Word we stand at all times in the sight of God. The all-seeing eye of the Almighty is upon us. We are under the divine obligation of faithfulness to Him. This is the obligation from above.

The obligation from without. This was the debt of which Paul wrote in Romans 1:14: "I am debtor both to Greeks and to Barbarians, both to the wise and to the foolish." Because he felt in a very personal way this responsibility, he could say: "I am ready to preach the gospel to you, also, that are in Rome." May God grant that each of us will hear the call of the lost and feel that that call is directed toward us. May we give the answer God has given us in His word. Hear the words of John as he spoke of our position in the world: "Even as He was in the world, so are ye" (I John 4:17). Why was Jesus in the world? His own answer is: "For the Son of man came to seek and to save the lost" (Luke 19:10). Not only was He ordained of God for His earthly mission, but He also heard the call from without. May our Father give us that same passion for souls.

The obligation from within. This is the feeling of personal indebtedness both to God and the lost. It is the work of the Spirit of God to "convict men of sin" through the Word. This He will do for you if you will let Him speak to you through His Word. The man of God cannot read even as much as one chapter in the Bible without seeing somewhere in that chapter the appeal of God to the lost. Yes, and more, he will likewise see that only through the instrumentality of men can this appeal, can this love, can this forgiveness of God, be made known; and *the minister is the instrument of God* for this purpose.

The greatest condemnation in hell belongs to those who misuse this sacred trust. Read James 3:1 and Luke 12:47. If there are measures of punishment in hell then the most agonizing of ﹒ affliction must be reserved for that minister who, through neglect fulness, the lust for other things, or through ignorance perverts his ministry. Preacher friend, there are *various* ways of misusing this sacred trust. Here are some of them:

Misusing our time. That is, devoting the time we have as men of God to the accomplishing of other things than those related to the great task of preaching the Word. I believe we would be safe in saying that the time spent by a minister of God should all be spent toward the end of either *preparing for* or *preaching* the word of Life. How much time do you waste each day? Let us realize that such a practice is *sin.*

Misusing our purpose. What is the purpose of the true minister of Christ Jesus? There can be but one purpose — the purpose of Christ Himself...to "glorify the Father who is in Heaven." And yet, how many of us have seen preachers ascend the platform to glorify themselves, their learning, the congregation to which they preach, their family, and sometimes even to glorify their own humility? May God deliver us from all such purposes; so let the words of Christ mean to us what He meant them to when He said: "If any man would come after me, let him deny himself..." (Matt. 16:24).

Misusing the message through perversion. Study carefully Matt. 23:13–28. Let the full significance of this scripture sink into your innermost heart. Please take note that Jesus is speaking of men much like you and me — men who were teachers of God's people, men who had studied His Word, those who were recognized as the spiritual leaders of the day. Jesus said of them that they were: "Sons of hell" (vs. 15b), "blind guides" (vs. 16), "fools" (vs. 17), "blind" (vs. 19), "hypocrites" (vs. 23), and "full of hypocrisy and iniquity" (vs. 28).

Is it possible for the minister to become a "son of hell" and by his teaching make more "sons of hell"? Can he be "blind," a "blind guide," a "fool," and a "hypocrite"? If he perverts the message of God by an inconsistent life, if he adds to the divine message human traditions and teaches them as the Word of God, then it is more than possible. Notice the case cited by Jesus. It has to do with swearing or taking oaths. God had laid down specific laws concerning the taking of oaths. See Lev. 19:12; Num. 32. The Pharisees accepted this law, *but* they thought it necessary to *help* God by way of adding their tradition or interpretation (Matt. 15:7-9), and teaching it as of equal value as the law itself. For this Jesus condemned them. Forget not that the Pharisees were charged with two counts: first, an inconsistent life; second, adding to the law of God. In addition to these traditions to the law of God, they also subtracted from God's word its true use and substituted for its purpose. May we come to feel that if we teach "our traditions" as the law of God the description of these teachers of old fits us like the shroud of death.

2. *We should know and realize the possibilities of the task.*

The possibility of pleasing God. When a husband truly loves his wife he will do almost anything to please her. Just to see the expression of surprise and joy in her eyes, to hear the words of appreciation and delight are all he needs to go to the furthest extent to please the one he so dearly loves. And just so, when we truly love God, then it will be our highest joy to please Him. When we contemplate all He is and all He has done for us in "The Beloved," can we do less than love Him? Are you seeking with all your heart to preach in just such a way and manner as to please our Heavenly Father? May we examine our hearts on this matter?

The possibility of shaping the lives and destinies of men and women. As a man "thinketh in his heart so is he" (Prov. 23:7). Now mark this: What a man thinks concerning God, Christ, salvation, happiness, hope and heaven, is largely determined by what you bring to him in your preaching. "Oh," you say, "he has a Bible. Let him read and study as well as hear." We may as well face the sad fact that the majority of people are going to take *our* word as the word of authority because they do not read the Bible. May we ever so speak that should they search the scriptures they would indeed find what we preached was what God has said. Whether the hearts of folk are filled with vibrant hope or vapid theology is very largely your responsibility.

Hitler sat behind his dictatorial desk and with a flourish of the hand and a few spoken words determined the destiny of thousands of anxious prisoners of war. Those persons were held behind barbed wire and prison walls. They were to be condemned or delivered according to the "Fuehrer's" word. Would you have freed these prisoners? Yea, would you? Then know this. You face each time you arise to preach some who are in the prison house of sin. Their eternal destinies are determined by what you say and how you say it. Responsibility? Possibilities? Think of it.

The possibility of making yourself into the likeness of our Saviour. J. H. Jowett had something very pointed to say on this thought in his book *"The Preacher and His Preaching,"* page 46:

> "A man may live in mountain country and lose all sense of the heights. And that is a terrible impoverishment, when mountain country comes to have the ordinary significance of the plains. So with the preacher. He may live among the cloud-capped mysteries of redeeming grace and lose all sense of the heights."

But such things need not be so; yea, matters can be reversed. We can find the great mountain peaks of God's wisdom and love. We can not only point others to the way, but can lead the way for them. We can have the glorious experience of growing in the grace and knowledge of our Lord and Saviour. But this blessing can be ours only if we keep a tender sensitiveness in our hearts toward God's Word and our task in the world.

This, then, is your possibility. May God grant that we will use it with a tender heart and not abuse it through carelessness.

3. *We should know and realize something of the divinity of the task.*

We have a divine message. It is of utmost importance to realize that the message we bring is divine. Do you feel as you preach the gospel that what you speak is the edict of eternity? Do you have the message of heaven? If we do we shall be reverent, careful and often in prayer as we open our mouth to preach. This impression of the divine nature of our message must ever be with us to keep us from degenerating into "just another speaker."

We have a divine power. There have been several queens in history who were said to be "the power behind the throne." Who is the power behind the pulpit? Is it the man you see standing there? I say no. There is another and better power in the man of God. The strength that counts for God is not his own. It is the power of God's eternal Spirit. The true man of God realizes, as none other, his own weakness, his necessary dependence upon God for strength. It is here that we can "by the Spirit put to death the deeds of the body" (Rom. 8:18). It is when we prepare to preach that we seek to be "strengthened with might by His Spirit in the inner man" (Eph. 3:16).

We have a divine reward. Think of it a moment. Yours is the inexpressible privilege of being the one to break upon the understanding of some precious soul the news of salvation; to see the knowledge of that soul's need asserting itself; to see the anxious expression on the face, the intense soberness of attitude and remark. Then it may be your joy one glad day to see that same one step out to come to the feet of Jesus; to grip the hand and with that handclasp feel the very pulsation of the heart; to think for a moment in your own heart of the question that is about to fall from your lips; to know in your innermost self that nothing you could ever say would be of greater importance: "Do you believe that Jesus is the Christ, the son of the living God?" and then, to stand by the grave of this one who has responded to the Word. Oh, it is a watery grave, true, but a grave none-the-less. You can then lead this penitent sinner out into the water, to there lower him into the grave. As you thus bury him you can look into the face of the object of Jesus' love. You can watch the water cover the old man, then gently lift from the water a new man, a new creature, a new life, a new child of God in Christ Jesus. This, my brothers, is one of the divine rewards of preaching. As someone has said, "All this and heaven too." What a joy!

May our God-arouse us to a new vision of our task and with this vision burning before us, may we go forth to conquer.

Questions for Self-examination. (Answer these questions from memory. Write your answers out in full. Do this for your own spiritual help; not just for the grade.)

1. What was the priceless possession of David, Moses and Elijah? How does this possession relate to the preacher of today?

2. What is the difference between "knowing and realizing"?

3. What does it mean to you that you are "God's man"?

4. What is the first thing we should know and realize concerning the task of preaching the Word?

5. State in your own words why you know that the position of the minister of the Word is greater than that of the presidency of the United States. If you do not believe this, state *why* you do not believe it.

6. How is it that you as a minister provide for man's hope, happiness and eternal life? Maybe you feel that you do not. If not, why not?

7. How are we as ministers obligated to God in a very real way?

8. Define in your own words the obligation from without.

9. How does I John 4:17 apply to us?

10. Explain in your own words *your* obligation from within.

11. Explain in detail Luke 12:47.

12. What is meant by "perverting your ministry"?

13. How is time perverted?

14. Mention three ways our purpose could be perverted.

15. Show how Matt. 23:13–28 applies to the perversion of the message.

16. State the three possibilities of preaching.

17. How would you go about pleasing God in your preaching?

18. How does the general neglect of the Bible lay a heavier burden upon the man of God?

19. What preacher is a greater sinner than the "Fuehrer"? (Do you believe this experimentally or intellectually?)

20. What do the words of Jowett mean to you?

21. What is the one essential requisite in growing in the grace and likeness of our Saviour?

22. How can it be said that we have a divine message?

23. Can we truly say we have a divine message when we prepare and deliver it in our own words?

24. Explain the operation of the divine power through preaching.

25. Tell in your own words what the salvation of one soul through your preaching would mean to you.

Assignment Four

Another examination of our motives as they relate to the goals toward which the man of God should aim in his preaching.

Answer *Yes* or *No*, then consider the percentage of your answer. *Suggestions:*

a. This could be done at home by each student; then the teacher could ask for the answers in class.

b. Each student should answer every question; the teacher could then select the questions he felt the most fruitful of help and discussion.

1. Will my preparation for preaching be such that I will know more and more of God's will?

Yes?————— No?————— Percentage?—————

Remember, in your preparation for preaching you can become a "topical artist" instead of a Bible student.

2. In my preparation will I ever seek to not only know the scriptures, but my own heart as well?

3. Knowing the deceitfulness of my heart (Jer. 17:9), will I always have my own heart in tune with what I preach before I preach it?

Remember, there is a big difference in preaching from experience and preaching from theory.

4. "I never call upon the community. I feel that is the task of the eldership." So said a certain preacher to me. Would you ever entertain such an idea? If you have never spoken to your folk in their living room, how can you speak to them in the meeting house?

5. Do you think you could learn to preach in a logical manner without the study of orderly thinking?

6. Is logical presentation essential to effective preaching?

7. If the understanding and use of the principles of orderly thinking requires much time and effort on your part, are you willing to pay the price?

8. If we have spoken ever so clearly and scripturally and yet no one is moved to obey, have you accomplished anything? ————————. If so, what?

O my soul, what goal hast thou in thine utterance?

9. There sits a man outside of Christ. He is hiding behind some "refuge of lies." Will you care enough to lead him out into the full glory of the gospel?

10. Next to the sinner out of Christ there sits one who has been a Christian for years — but he needs food — and that desperately. Will you send him away hungry?

11. Will you truly attempt to move men and women to "love and good works"?

12. In the rear pew there is seated the back-slider — back-slider in heart; the thorns of the world in his heart have choked out the Word. Can you remove these thorns and still not damage the heart beyond repair?

My dear brother, know that there is more to preaching than preparing a scriptural address to be delivered in a logical form.

Assignment Five

a. Read the following discussion.

b. Do this with the thought of your own personal relationship to the subject.

c. After reading the discussion, from memory answer the questions which follow.

Some of the goals toward which the man of God should aim in his preaching.

1. *He should preach with knowledge.*

He should preach with a knowledge of the scriptures.

This might seem rather superfluous to some, but it is not! If every minister that is now preaching in a located pastorate were required to give in five paragraphs the contents of the first five books of the Old Testament or in the same number of paragraphs the outline of the life of Christ, what would the result be? There is nothing more important to the man of God than a thorough homiletical knowledge of the entire Bible. You will note that I said *homiletical knowledge.* It is one thing to know the content of the Bible (which all too few do) and quite another thing to have a grasp of the Bible from a preaching viewpoint. There are a number of good sets of books that I do not hesitate to recommend as an aid to this type of knowledge. They are: *The Biblical Illustrator; The Pulpit Commentary; The Expositor's Bible; Homiletical Thesaurus.*

It should be our purpose to preach God's word; not to preach about the Bible, but to *preach the Word.* Someone has aptly said concerning the illustration of the sermon that the Word itself could furnish us thoroughly unto this good work.

Let us then place before us the goal of so preparing to preach that we, through this preparation, will be personally acquainted in word and truth of the contents of the oracles of Jehovah.

We should preach with a knowledge of our own hearts. "For I say, through the grace that was given me, to every man that is among you, not to think of himself more highly than he ought to think; but so to think as to think soberly, according as God hath dealt to each man a measure of faith" (Romans 12:3). So did Paul write to the saints in Rome. My, how the principle herein applies to preachers! So often are we tempted to think of ourselves more highly than we ought to think. If we will but take the place of a sinner saved by grace, we will best be able to preach to the needs of others. Why is it that we cannot think "soberly" at all times? We must be completely honest with ourselves, to be conscious of our inabilities, weaknesses and sins every day, and not only in the day of adversity.

Preaching is an act of worship (Acts 2:42). Therefore it should be performed by the preacher in the most reverent attitude. Can you truly pray without thinking of your heart condition? Even as your prayers are given to God in the presence of God so may we preach in His presence. This should be something of our self-knowledge.

We should preach with a knowledge of the hearts of those to whom we preach. Do we really care? Do we care above the approval of men? Why do we preach to folk? We say it is because we want them to become Christians or if they are, we want them, by our preaching, to become better Christians. But what would you think of a doctor who had one remedy, one treatment for all human ills? What would you think of a doctor who never made a diagnosis? What, then, do you think of a preacher who preaches to persons he does not know? To individuals among whom he has lived for months and years and yet he knows not the problems of their hearts? This is inexcusable. This is not a true shepherd. He cares not for the sheep but for his own selfish, personal interests. How can we speak to the hearts of those who hear us if we know not their hearts? Charles Finney in his book *Revivals of Religion* has a very pointed comment upon this thought:

> "A minister ought to know the religious opinions of every sinner in his congregation. Indeed, a minister in the country is generally inexcusable if he does not. He has no excuse for not knowing the religious views of all his congregation and of all that may come under his influence if he has had opportunity to know them. How, otherwise, can he preach to them? How can he know how to bring forth things new and old and adapt truth to their case?" (Pages 190–191).

2. *He should preach logically.* Two women were overheard discussing a third person (this is sometimes called gossip). One of the statements made concerning a conversation that one of these women had with the third person could well be applied to many a sermon. She said, "Well, you know as we were talking one thing led to another." One thing led to another. That is the exact description of some sermons. No real attempt at beginning, development, or conclusion. There is one thing that this disjointed discourse will never lead to and that is the salvation of souls or the edifying of Christians. Unless we know where we are going and how we are going to get there, how shall we be able to lead others? An effective sermon has a definite beginning, development and conclusion.

3. *He should aim to preach convincingly.* In the sight of God there are but three great spiritual classes of individuals. They are the sinner, the saint, and the backslider. These same classes will be in attendance where you preach. Your task? To *convince* them of their need and of Christ's remedy.

Will you take careful note of the following words: Persuade (Acts 17:4); Beseech (II Cor. 5:20); Convict (Acts 2:37); Exhort (Titus 1:9); Reprove; Rebuke (II Timothy 4:2).

These are all words that describe the *manner* in which the gospel was preached in the days of the Apostles. Unless you are willing to become so absorbed in the subject of preaching, so in love with people that you want to persuade, beseech, exhort, reprove, rebuke, convict as you preach you do not have the true goal before you as a preacher. I hope you are reading this after a season of prayer so the truth of these words will penetrate your heart.

Questions for Self-examination. (Answer these questions from memory. Write your answers out in full. Do this for your own spiritual help, not just for a grade.)

1. What are the three great goals toward which the man of God should aim in his preaching?

2. What is meant by knowing the Scriptures in relation to preaching?

3. Could you give an outline of the first five books of the Bible or of the life of Christ? Do you honestly feel this has anything to do with your ability to preach effectively?

4. Do you think that the suggestion made concerning the illustrations of the sermon was a practical one? You plan on using it? If not, why not?

5. Getting down to practical cases; how should a minister prepare his sermons so as to become a Bible student?

6. What is meant by thinking "soberly" of ourselves? Answer this as if you were teaching another what you believe.

7. What was Finney's comment on knowing those to whom you speak? What did you think of it?

8. If you were the only doctor for five hundred sick folk, would you try to diagnose each case before treatment? What is the application of this to preaching?

9. Would preaching with logic not destroy the leading of the Holy Spirit? If not, why not? If so, how?

10. Is it necessary to make every sermon one that convinces? Have we failed if we do not convince? If so, how much? If not, why not?

Assignment Six

A Personal Spiritual Aptitude Test for Preachers. (Answer these at home and discuss your answers in class.)

1. Do you believe there is a definite method that can be learned for using the Scriptures in sermon preparation? Yes?———— No?———— Explain your answer ————

———————————————————

2. What type of hindrance would the lack of method in sermon preparation be? Choose one: a. A hindrance to definite decisions. b. A hindrance to expression of thought. c. A hindrance to scriptural presentation.

3. Do you personally feel that it is a "privilege" to preach? If so, in what way?

4. What does "love" have to do with the motive for preaching?

5. Do you believe this statement: "The world has yet to see what God could do with a life that is totally surrendered to Him"? Do you propose to be that man?

6. What is your definition of "prejudice"?

7. Do you think it would be possible to be prejudiced against God? If so, how? Are you?

8. Is it totally wrong to try to imitate another preacher?

9. What is the danger in imitation?

10. Does heredity and environment have anything to do with success or failure as a preacher? If so, to what degree?

11. Are there fellows now studying for the ministry that should be told that they will never make a success of the ministry and therefore should seek another field of service?

12. Do you feel that it is a "sin" not to pray or just one of the many ways that we could improve?

13. Does a man have a right to speak for Jesus in public who will not speak for Him in private?

14. Do you know the meaning of the following words: Lasciviousness, licentiousness, uncleanness; i.e., in their Biblical connotation? Would it be possible for a minister to partake of these sins and yet remain undetected by his congregation? Do modern day magazines and movies contribute to these sins?

15. What are the indications of a "vain" minister? What are the causes? What is the remedy?

Assignment Seven

> Read the following discussion. Answer from memory the questions which follow.

The Man of God should have a Life that is free for Service.

1. Free from the binding power of ignorance.

What a fetter is ignorance, but never more so than when related to the use of the Scripture in sermon making. We have already spoken of the general lack of scriptural knowledge, but of the two deficiencies the one we are now considering is the greater. You have probably known men who were somewhat versed in the Word of God, and yet possessed no real knowledge of how to use the Bible in sermon preparation. It is one thing to know the Word, but it is quite another to be able to use that same knowledge in truth in such a way that it will lend itself to a basis for a sermon or a lesson. There are definite principles of homiletics that should be used to the glory of God by every minister who wants to be God's man. May this course of study serve to remedy to some extent this lack.

I think of another form of ignorance and its binding power. Have you ever stepped into the glorious liberty of the exhilaration that comes with doing something for the sheer joy of doing it? The preacher who preaches because he has a job to discharge or a duty to perform is terribly bound. He should read the scriptures long enough to catch the sense of privilege Paul felt in preaching. Webster defines privilege as being "peculiar advantage or right." This indeed it is when related to preaching the gospel. It will become this to us when we love Christ and those for whom Christ died.

There is the fetter of hesitancy for fear of failure. This, too, stems from ignorance. "The world has yet to see what God could do with one life totally surrendered to Him." In most human efforts the axiom "You will never know until you try" is applicable. In the ministry it is also true, but our trying is of no avail without our surrender. So it is more true to say, "You will never know until you have tried in surrender." May we be able to pray the united prayer: "Oh God, strike from our hands all shackles of hesitancy, selfishness or doubt; help us to put ourselves into your hands that by our preparation, perspiration and your divine superintendence we will be the kind of men you want us to be."

2. *Free from the binding power of prejudice.*

Some brothers would fain rather be made in the image and likeness of some successful preacher than they would in the image and likeness of Jehovah. This I believe to be a form of that sin "worse than idolatry" designated in the oracles as "covetousness." What is covetousness but lusting after that which is the property of another. Like it or not, the personality of another is his peculiar property and it can never be yours. The only thing one can secure by this type of covetousness is a certain sensation of trying to use something that is not yours and that you know not how to use. This mistake of imitation will result in a glaring caricature of the real thing. Like the caricature such an effort will emphasize the weak points rather than the strong ones.

Thinking a little further on this matter we see that it has serious complications. If we try to imitate the personality of another, are we not reflecting on the wisdom of God for making us like we are? If you are dissatisfied with your station in life this dissatisfaction can lead to something very good or very bad. If you will take your need to Jesus who can "make all things new," to let Him be formed within you "from glory to glory" (a gradual change), then the dissatisfaction is a blessing in disguise. But if you look through carnal eyes to the lives of others and "wish I were Mr. So and So" whether it be a wistful thought or an effort of imitation, you are prejudiced against God. This is true because *prejudice is that conclusion reached by any person upon any subject without a thorough consideration of all the evidence.* If we would consider *all* the evidence presented in God's book we would find that God has created each one of us as His "peculiar treasure" and He is so vitally interested in each one of us that no one need feel at all slighted.

3. *Free from the binding power of hidden sin.*

"God forbid that I should sin against God by ceasing to pray for you" (I Sam. 12:23). So spoke God's prophet Samuel in the long ago. And so should the man of God speak today. We should not think of the failure to pray in the public assembly for we are seldom guilty there. But can we say of our congregation, "God forbid that I should sin against God by ceasing to pray for you"? In the quiet of my study, in the busy daily routine, God forbid that I should sin against God by ceasing to pray for you. Say brother, are you a sinner in this matter? If you never spoke to your wife about your concern over your children any more often than you speak to your God over your concern for the souls entrusted to you, could you convince your wife that you really cared for your children? A sign has been nailed to many a wall which reads: "Prayer is Power." How many a minister has walked into the building and upon seeing the sign said to himself or out loud, "Yes, yes, how true that is," when all the time his life was void of power for the very reason that in the solitude of self with God he sinned because he neglected to pray!

It is indeed passing strange that the same preacher who pleads so earnestly for the souls of men from the pulpit, if placed along side those same precious souls in personal contact, will treat them as if he did not care. The same evangelist who so fervently prays and preaches for the salvation of the lost in the public does not say a word to the lost one beside him on the bus or train, or to those who have lived next door to him "at home." I say there is something wrong with such a man. It can be nothing short of a failure in motives. We have been seeking the approval of men and not of God. When we are placed in the company of sinners who are not at the moment interested in hearing of Christ, rather than face a little disapproval or disinterest, or a little deflating of the ego, we keep quiet. When it is the popular thing to do, when we have the floor and everyone is for us, then how bold we do become. From all such hypocrisy, O God, deliver us.

There are certain words that we do not like to hear too often because of their implications. Such words are "lasciviousness," "licentiousness" and "uncleanness." All of these words, as used in God's word, involve the mind and relate to sins of the mind or heart. The same sin Jesus spoke of when He said: "He that looketh on a woman to lust after her, hath committed adultery already with her in his heart." If there is anything that would bind the hands and heart of the man of God it would be this sin. While we are in this present world the flesh is going to lust against the spirit and the spirit against the flesh, for these two are contrary the one to the other (Gal. 5:17). Paul spoke of this warfare in the seventh chapter of Romans, *but* he thanked God for deliverance through Jesus Christ our Lord. Where is this deliverance to be found? At the throne of grace — to this throne in prayer we are to come in our time of need that we might receive *grace* and *mercy* to help us. Our living, loving Father assures us that His grace is sufficient for us, and that His strength is perfected or made known to us in our weakness. But this can never be true unless we are willing to come to the place of appropriation.

The reason the battle against desire or lust is lost is because it is fought out in the solitude of self and Satan. There can be only *one* outcome to such a contest — defeat. But the same problem carried daily, hourly, to the throne of grace can and will be solved in glorious freedom and victory.

Questions for Self-examination. (Answer these questions at home and discuss the answers in class.)

1. How does covetousness enter into the effort of imitation?

2. What will be the result of the wrong type of imitation?

3. What did Paul mean when he said, "imitate me"?

4. When is it helpful to become dissatisfied with our personality?

5. What is prejudice?

6. How does the man born blind (John 9:1-41) become an example to us in accepting God's will?

7. Would it be possible to hold a prejudice in the realm of the influence of heredity on our personalities? If so, how?

8. Is it a sin not to pray? How do you know? A sin against whom?

9. What is the underlying cause of a failure of personal testimony?

10. How can we win in the battle of the lust of the flesh?

SUGGESTED READING

Jowett, J. H. *The Preacher His Life and Work.* p. 41-71.
Bounds, E. M. *The Preacher and Prayer.* Chapters 1-3.
Hogue, Wilson T. *Homiletics and Pastoral Theology.* p. 291-306.

Chapter 2
The Definition of the Sermon

THE ACHING HEART

The world's great heart is aching, aching fiercely in the night,
And God alone can heal it, and God alone give light;
And the men to bear the message, and to preach the living Word,
Are you and I, my brothers, and all others that have heard.

Can we close our eyes in slumber, can we fold our hands at ease,
While the gates of night stand open to the pathway of the seas?
Can we shut up our compassion, can we leave one prayer unsaid,
Ere the souls that sin has ruined have been wakened from the
dead?

We grovel among trifles, and our spirits fret and toss,
While above us burns the vision of the Christ upon the cross,
And the blood of God is dropping from his wounded hands
and side,
And the voice of God is crying, "Tell poor sinners I have died!"

O Voice of God, we hear thee, above the wrecks of time,
Thine echoes roll around us, and the message is sublime;
No power of men shall thwart us, no stronghold us dismay,
For God commands obedience, and love has led the way!

Chapter 2

THE DEFINITION OF THE SERMON

At the outset of this chapter it might be well to define the important terms of our subject. The word "sermon" has its root in the Latin language. The Latin word "sermo" means "a discourse"; thus from the etymology of the word we understand that a sermon is a discourse. Yea, but the best sermons are far more than just a discourse in a church service.

What is the relationship of homiletics to the sermon? *Homiletics is the art of preparing and delivering a sermon.* Many times have I listened to certain persons poke fun at the seemingly superfluous subject of homiletics. I take no offense at such remarks for most of the time they are made in the spirit of harmless jest. However, on occasions I have felt there has been a misconception of the true meaning of homiletics. Think for a moment (that rare exercise), if homiletics is the art of preparing and delivering sermons, does it seem reasonable that we should neglect it? Are not all preachers engaged in that very art? There is a limited definition of homiletics that is currently popular among some that homiletics consists of learning how best to say "firstly, secondly, and thirdly." The man who has studied homiletics will be very careful to make his sermons logically symmetrical. This is no fault in itself, but the mechanics of forming an outline can be over emphasized. Homiletics is the *art* of preparing and delivering a sermon. All the best information on how to prepare a sermon, both from sacred and profane sources, is studied in a true course on the subject. Any notion that homiletics is dry or stuffy or a sort of necessary evil should be forever removed by a knowledge of the true meaning of this wonderful essential subject.

Assignment Eight

Simple stimulating questions for you to answer before you prepare a sermon.

1. What is the best definition you can give of a sermon? Make it original.

2. Should a sermon ever be read? If not, why not? If so, when?

3. What makes a sermon "seem too long"? (Come now. Do not be diplomatic. Answer this question in a candid helpful way.)

4. What would you estimate is the average age intelligence of the audience to whom you are going to speak?

5. Give three definite reasons why some people cannot understand some preachers. Who is at fault? Develop this question from the responsibility of the preacher.

6. What happens when a message is "too obvious"? Is this a sin? How shall we remedy this?

7. How is the man of God going to help society? By the "social gospel"? If so, in what way? If not, why not?

8. What would be your definition of "religion" as it relates to preaching?

9. How could Matt. 15:9 apply to modern day preaching? How does the use of inference have a part in this?

10. Why do some preachers avoid some subjects? Is this wise? Is this preaching the whole council of God?

Assignment Nine

> Read the following discussion on the subject and answer
> the questions.

In our definition of a sermon we are using the one given by Austin Phelps:

> "A sermon is an oral address to the popular mind, upon a religious truth, as contained in the scriptures, elaborately treated, with a view to persuasion." *Theory of Preaching*.

You will note that there are *six parts* to this definition. We will deal with each one separately.

1. *A sermon is an "oral" address.*

This being true it should be given complete verbal freedom. Read carefully this quotation from Dean Brown:

> "There is no other calling where a man making a popular appeal trusts for his results to a carefully read paper. The lawyer does not stand before his jury with a paper even

though it might have been written in style which combined all the excellence of Blackstone and of Edmund Burke. The political orator campaigning for votes would not mount the bustlings with a paper to be read even though the address were written in Addison's best English and the thought as profound as Plato's republic. None of these men would insulate himself by a thick pile of paper from those with whom he would make connections and to whom he would impart himself by some mysterious electric current. . . . And they attempt this harder task of uttering their words without manuscript to obtain "a corruptible crown." *The Art of Preaching,* pages 81–82.

To be an effective oral address the sermon should have the element of *direct address;* this it cannot have if it is read from a manuscript.

There have been a few rare souls who have, despite the disadvantages of reading the sermon, made a success out of this practice. But this is surely the exception, not the rule.

A sermon is an "oral address," but what type of an *oral* address?

"It is a clear advantage for a man to cultivate the habit of using a pleasant tone of voice always. If his ordinary mode of speech is harsh, husky, rasping or shrill, it will be almost impossible for him to display that quality of tone suitable for the conveyance of a message of spiritual help. If a man's words say one thing and his voice says another, he is working at cross purposes. If his language invites and his tones repel, the people will go far toward robbing his work of its power. Every public speaker might well talk for five or ten minutes in his usual style into a graphophone which will reproduce for him with amazing fidelity those inflections and infelicities of tone production which many a waiting congregation has found a burden grievous to be borne. He will there behold his natural self in a glass and knowing what manner of man he is vocally, he may be moved to go his way and strive for a better quality of voice." *The Art of Preaching,* pages 164–165.

One final quotation:

"The steady monotone, sometimes known among the ungodly as the 'preaching tone' will make any sermon seem long." — The man who is *uniformly* earnest, *uniformly* tender, *uniformly* emphatic; the man who is striving to say something appealing and helpful with every breath he draws, becomes wearisome. The conversational method wears better than any other because it has in it more of the element of variety and because it also strikes more effectually the human note." *The Art of Preaching*, pages 110–111.

We will have more to say on the proper use of the voice in our chapter on the delivery of the sermon.

2. *It is addressed "to the popular mind."*

It has been estimated that the intelligence of your average listener is that of a twelve-year-old. Be that as it may (and I have my doubts about it), the lack of intelligent Biblical information is appalling. When we say a sermon is addressed to the "popular mind" it is with this so-called "average" listener we are dealing. The majority of persons listening have no understanding whatsoever of theological terms or ecclesiastical verbiage. We can accommodate what Paul wrote to the Corinthians: "In the church I would rather speak five words with understanding than ten thousand words in an unknown tongue" (I Cor. 14:19). The "unknown tongue" we employ has been acquired under the lamp of our study and most of your listeners have never been to that far off country.

But then the message is not understood or appreciated by "the popular mind" for other reasons. Sometimes the message is "hazy or foggy" in thought. The fundamental difficulty here is with the purpose of the sermon. The preacher does not have a clear conception of this thought nor how he wants to express it. The more he talks the more complicated and confusing it becomes.

Then there is the preacher who tells you all his conclusions without bothering to say how he obtained them. When this man begins to elaborate on these conclusions, it really misses the "popular mind."

On the other hand, we should be very careful that we do not become too obvious in our preaching. If I may be permitted a personal word, I want to say that there is no type of preaching that so irritates me as this type. If one mistake is committed more often than another in reaching the popular mind, this must be at the top of the list.

"The sermon is made to seem unduly long by the man who dwells on the obvious. It may be necessary now and then for a public speaker to say that two and two make four. It is not necessary, however, to enlarge upon that statement and rub it in, or to illustrate it, or to exhort the people to put their trust in it. The moment such a truth is uttered, the people are saying, 'We know that.' We feel the full force of it. Now what comes of it? What bearing has it upon the problems of life as we face them? Proceed at once to what follows.

"It may be appropriate now and then for a preacher to say that the sun rose yesterday morning in the east and on time as usual. This is a perfectly sound statement; it would be regarded as sound even at Princeton. But the people are only interested in knowing what comes of it. The fact itself is instantly apparent without further effort on the part of the man who makes the reference. Now let him get down to business and make some worthy use of what is so entirely obvious.

"Unless you are unfolding some *old truth* in *a new way*, or *making a fresh application of some old truth* to change conditions or by your *vital interpretation* of it, causing that old truth to live over again in the hearts of your people, you are in a fair way to bore your congregation. You will rob them of their time to no purpose when you needlessly dwell upon that which is undeniably old and familiar. The man who dwells even for three minutes on some perfectly obvious truth will cause the people to feel that he has been preaching to them for a full half hour." *The Art of Preaching*, pages 108–109.

3. *It is based "upon a religious truth."*

What is a religious truth? There are some realms of truth that are non-religious. Facts are facts wherever they are found. The preacher of the gospel should deal in *religious truth*, not philosophical or social or biographical truths, except as these are a part of the religious truth he is committed to preach.

Certainly the gospel we preach should enter and affect the social life of the individual, but to place the emphasis upon the social aspect is to finally fail in binding men back to God. The only way to a social change that is Christ-like is through the change of heart.

And as to overemphasize in the field of biography, we can say "The lives of great men *do* remind us that we can make our lives sublime, and in passing leave behind us footprints in the sands of time." (Cf. *The Psalm of Life* by Longfellow.) But the lives of great men were and are only great because of their exercising of obedience to the laws of God and His Son, whether they recognize it or not. Hence it would indeed be foolish to emphasize and eulogize the result rather than the cause.

Philosophy is a mighty subject and within its scope many a noble thought can be found. Most of all would I say a word of commendation for Christian philosophy. But the pulpit is no place for a discussion of philosophical principles per se. God is the true source of all wisdom and knowledge (Jas. 1:5); and in Christ are all the treasures of wisdom and knowledge hidden (Col. 2:3). It is perfectly possible to act upon the principles of Christian philosophy without a knowledge of its internal structure.

4. *Let us preach the Word "as contained in the Scriptures."*

It does seem unnecessary of emphasis that a minister of the gospel should prepare his sermon "upon a religious truth as contained in the Scriptures." But mark well this thought:

a. *We can add to the Scriptures by inference.* If the inference is a primary and fair deduction, one that does not violate any other passage of scripture, it would be well to use it. But there are so many inferences drawn from the scriptures that are nothing but the opinions of men. We have accepted as true some thought that has been presented to us, not being able to find any plain statement of scripture to support it, we "infer" its support from the Bible. Let me say very plainly—if you teach your deductions and inferences as the Word of God you are as guilty as the Pharisee that Jesus condemned. Yea, and of the *same sin.* (Cf. Matt. 15:7–9.)

b. *We can subtract from the Word by theory.* This is the antithesis of what we have just said. In this instance the Word is not added to, but *diluted.* We read a passage that puzzles us because it diametrically opposes our creed. We know it cannot mean what it seems to say so we use a process of rationalization which will subtract from the text every vestige of thought contrary to our preconceived theory or belief. We obtain our belief from second hand sources, not from the hand of God through our study of His Word, but from the hand of man and our study of his creed. Written or unwritten creeds are the works of men. Let us be brutally honest with ourselves on this matter.

c. *We can substitute for the Word because of personal desire or lust.* Actually, addition and subtraction are a form of substitution; but I have another thought to present. It is a strange but well established fact that man can find excuse for any sin committed. There is hardly a criminal behind bars today who would not excuse his crime through some pretense or another. Something of this same type of self-justification is used in relation to the Word of God. Rather than admit the personal cleansing, purifying power of the gospel, the preacher who is full of his own ways and desires will substitute for the strong gospel truth his evasions and vagaries. They come from a heart full of lust and desire to justify his disobedience to God's law.

So far we can say that a true sermon is that oral address to the average mind upon a religious truth as it is contained in the Scriptures, neither added to by inference, subtracted from by theory, nor substituted for by personal lust.

Assignment Ten

Answer the following questions from memory. Do this at home and discuss your answers in class.

1. Give, from memory, the complete definition of a sermon.

2. Do you accept the idea that verbal freedom is hindered by reading the sermon? If so, why? If not, why not?

3. Do you feel that "the conversational tone" in preaching would destroy the evangelistic message?

4. Will your sermon have to be "popular" to reach the popular mind?

5. What is the difficulty in "hazy or foggy" preaching?

6. Why is it a sin to be too obvious in our preaching? Can anything be *too clear?*

7. What is "religious truth" according to our use of the term?

8. Is it wrong to use biographies or social applications in our preaching? If so, why? If not, why not?

9. When is it right to use an inference and when is it wrong?

10. What are some of the reasons for men adding, subtracting, or substituting for the Word of God? Which reason would most tempt you?

Assignment Eleven

Speaking to the heart. These questions are intended to stir your conscience. Answer them accordingly.

1. "This brother is not much of a preacher, but he is a fine teacher." Do you accept this as a possibility? If so, why?

2. If a sermon does not touch the conscience of the listener, is it worthy of the name? Have the sermons you have heard in the last month all touched your conscience? Who is at fault if this is not so?

3. How is it that some material is made monotonous by repetition and some is not?

4. Should you have definite persons in mind when you prepare your message? If so, in what way should you have them in mind?

5. Is it really right to try to persuade someone to become a Christian? Is this not encroaching on the work of God and His Spirit?

6. Does fear have any place on our persuasion of men? If so, where?

7. Of what are we guilty if we do *not* preach persuasively?

8. Are there not some men whose temperaments are not at all fitted to persuasive preaching? Are they, then, responsible in the same manner as others?

9. Would it be right to measure the success of your ministry by the number of men and women who have been persuaded to accept Christ and live for Him?

10. Give the complete definition of a sermon. Remember, it has six parts.

Assignment Twelve

Read the following discussion of the last two parts to the sermon's definition.

5. It is to be "elaborately treated."

Perhaps there is a question in the mind of some just what is here meant. I take it to mean that a sermon should be more than a Biblical outline, more than a Bible study. It would be developed with a definite object in mind. This does not refer to the length of a sermon; a message may only be fifteen minutes long and yet be elaborately enough treated to accomplish its purpose. As a general observation I would say a message is elaborately treated when there is included in it Biblical teaching that helps both the listener and the preacher.

If those who attend the services where you preach do not take away with them some new application of truth already known, or some new truth they had not seen before, then your sermon is not a sermon in the truest and highest sense of the word.

When you prepare to go hunting I am sure you are careful to secure the best gun you can find, and the best ammunition. This is important, but the most important thing in hunting is to bring back the game. Just so when we preach. It is important to have a good outline that the material be understood; important that the scriptures be used, but it is *most* important that we seek to relate this outline and material to the lives of those who come. In your mind's eye gather around your study desk the members of your congregation. Consider each as an individual. What is his need? Then in that atmosphere prepare your sermon.

6. *It is to be constructed "with a view to persuasion."*

Paul said, concerning his ministry, "Knowing the fear of the Lord we persuade men" (II Cor. 5:11). It would follow then, would it not, that if we in our preaching fail to persuade men we lack something in our fear of the Lord? If we will prepare and preach our sermons in the light of eternity, either in hell or heaven, we will persuade men. We will speak "as a dying man to dying men." A sermon that is not prepared and preached with the purpose of action will not and can not result in action. If we do not "beseech men on behalf of Christ to be reconciled to God" we fail in this most important aspect of a sermon.

Questions for Self-examination. (Answer them at home, discuss your answers in class.)

1. When is a sermon more than a Biblical study or outline?
2. What is the ideal length for a sermon?
3. What is "interesting truth"? Or when is truth interesting?
4. How is preaching like hunting?
5. What mental imagery should the preacher employ as he prepares his sermon? This is for the purpose of being able to speak to the needs of the congregation.

6. If we fail to persuade men in our preaching, according to II Cor. 5:11, what is our lack?

7. What will cause us to speak as a dying man to dying men?

8. Why is a definite purpose in preaching so important?

9. Why is the sixth part of the definition of a sermon the most important?

10. Give from memory the six parts of the definition of a sermon.

A sermon is:

1. —————————————————————— ——————

2. ——————————————————————————

3. ——————————————————————————

4. ——————————————————————————

5. ——————————————————————————

6. ——————————————————————————

Think of the development behind each of these points and try to make it yours when you prepare and preach your sermons.

SUGGESTED READING

Broadus, John A. (Revised by Jesse Burton Weatherspoon) *On The Preparations and Delivery of Sermons.* p. 1–14.

Macartney, Clarence E. *Preaching Without Notes.* p. 9–30.

Morgan, G. Campbell. *Preaching.* p. 9–38.

Chapter 3

An Explanation of the Parts
of the Sermon Outline

ARE ALL THE CHILDREN IN?

Are all the children in? The night is falling,
 And storm clouds gather in the threatening west;
The lowing cattle seek a friendly shelter;
 The bird flies to her nest;
The thunder crashes; wilder grows the tempest,
 And darkness settles o'er the fearful din;
Come, shut the door, and gather round the hearthstone;
 Are all the children in?

Are all the children in? The night is falling,
 When gilded sin doth walk about the streets.
O, "at the last it biteth like a serpent!"
 Poisoned are stolen sweets.
O mothers, guard the feet of inexperience,
 Too prone to wander in the paths of sin!
O, shut the door of love against temptation!
 Are all the children in?

Are all the children in? The night is falling,
 The night of death is hastening on apace;
The Lord is calling, "Enter thou thy chamber,
 And tarry there a space."
And when he comes, the King in all his glory,
 Who died the shameful death our hearts to win,
O may the gates of heaven shut about us,
 With all the children in!

Chapter 3

AN EXPLANATION OF THE PARTS OF THE SERMON OUTLINE

INTRODUCTION

There are *seven* parts to a sermon outline. Here is a picture of a sermon showing the inter-relationship of its various parts.

TEXT
THEME
INTRODUCTION
PROPOSITION

Main Division   Main Division
Sub. Div. Sub. Div. Sub. Div.   Sub. Div. Sub. Div. Sub. Div.
Main Division
Sub. Div. Sub. Div. Sub. Div.

C O N C L U S I O N

You will note in the chart that the entire sermon is suspended upon the *text*. The theme grows out of the text, the introduction introduces the proposition from the theme. Upon the proposition is suspended the main and subdivisions. The conclusion concludes in such a way as to relate back to the proposition and at the same time embrace the main and subdivisions.

But we are a bit ahead of our sequence of thought. Will you do this assignment before we launch into the details of the sermon outline?

Assignment Thirteen

(A Test of Your Analytical Powers)

1. From John 14:1–6 select one verse as a possible text for a sermon. Answer the following questions about your selection:

Why did you select the particular verse you did?

(1) Because it was the condensed thought of the whole passage?

(2) Because it appealed to you as being especially true?

(3) Because you felt you could apply it to life?

(Select the answer in those above nearest to your reason and enlarge upon it or tell the full reason for your selection.)

2. From the verse you chose in John 14:1–6 what thought do you hope to develop? Select the one from the following list that is nearest to your "thought" or "theme" for your sermon:

(1) The troubled heart and its cure.
(2) Belief in God.
(3) Jesus the Christ.
(4) My Father's house.
(5) The many mansions.
(6) The truthfulness of Jesus.
(7) The certainty of heaven.
(8) Heaven a place.
(9) Heaven in preparation.
(10) Safe in the arms of Jesus.
(11) The second coming.
(12) The Way.
(13) How to know the Way.
(14) The Way, the Truth and the Life.
(15) The Way to heaven.

Restate in your own words the one you selected. Now *cut* your statement down to as few words as possible. If you can state it in *one* word, fine. Do it. Keep it terse, but make it forceful and as interesting as possible. Nothing dull in your theme, is there? If there is, it will not be dull to others; it will be *dead*.

3. State in one sentence (the shorter the better) what you hope to do with this theme. What do you aim to accomplish in your development? Make it specific. *Specify. Specify. No generalizations!* Make this statement contain *one* objective; not two or three or four or ten but *one*. Here it is. Fill in the blanks:

"In this theme I am going to ——————————

——————————————————

4. Now name *three* ways you are going to accomplish this purpose. You know what your purpose is; you have just stated it. Now *how* are you going to carry it out? Fill in the blanks:

(1) By ——————————————————————

(2) By ——————————————————————

(3) By ——————————————————————

5. Each of those ways you decide to use in developing your aim has an independent thought. How do you propose to develop it? Be careful. Remember the picture. Here it is with other names in it.

John 14:1–6

Your Theme

Your Aim from Your Theme

How you developed your aim.	How you developed your aim.	How you developed your aim.

Now your purpose is to develop each point under your aim so they will be separate of each other and yet will all develop your objective. Can you do it? Try it. Give two points of development under each thought. Write it out. Word it well. Pray about it. Make it good. Use it if you can in preaching.

Now your development looks like this:

John 14:1–6

Your Theme

Your Aim in Development

How you developed your aim.	How you developed your aim.	How you developed your aim.
1. Enlargement of development.	1. Enlargement of development.	1. Enlargement of development.
2. Same as above	2. Same as above	2. Same as above

If your development is not coherent, go back to your text and work down carefully until it is.

6. After you have completed your development you are ready to conclude the message. Can you do so in such a way as to result in action on the basis of what you have said? We will have more to say about the definite form of the conclusion in another chapter.

7. Have you noticed that we left out the introduction? We really never left it out. We have waited until we know just what we were going to introduce. Although the introduction stands between the theme and the proposition (third in order), it is best to wait until you at least have your outline formulated before you make your introduction. In this way you will know how best to formulate it.

We suggest that you take this test at home and bring your material to class to be helped by the class and the teacher.

Assignment Fourteen

Read the following discussion and answer the questions.

1. *The Text.*

The text is that portion of God's Word the minister selects to form the basis for his sermon.

It should, first of all, be clearly understood by both the preacher and the congregation. For this reason it is sometimes necessary to give an explanation of the text. Please never over estimate the Biblical knowledge of your audience. What might be very obvious to you is sometimes very obscure to them. It is almost always necessary to give a few words of explanation as to just how you have chosen to use this passage of scripture. Here are a couple of texts, one which would need explanation of context and the other would not. Can you tell which is which?

1. II Sam. 24:24.
2. Rom. 12:12.

Both scripture texts will need explanation as to how they are going to be used, but one of them needs an explanation as to its historical setting in order to be understood. The preacher and the audience must understand the text.

When Jesus went into the synagogue on the Sabbath Day He was given the book of the prophet Isaiah. He opened the book and found the place where it was written:

"The Spirit of the Lord is upon me, because he hath anointed me to preach good tidings to the poor; He hath sent me to proclaim release to the captives, and recovering of sight to the blind, to set at liberty them that are bruised, to preach the acceptable year of the Lord." Luke 4:18, 19.

Why did He read this portion of scripture? If you will read verse 21 of this same chapter you will know.

"And He began to say unto them, today hath this scripture been fulfilled in your ears."

If we cannot say this of the text we have chosen, we had best look for another. We must be able to see the direct relationship of the needs of the people and the text we have selected. It is only when we can feel the pulsation of the heart of the congregation in our sermon text that it truly becomes a sermon. It is only by saying in effect: "Today hath this scripture a fulfillment in you" that we can know we have a message from God to those who hear us.

The book of John is a wonderful book for texts. There are enough in it to keep us preaching for years. The book of Acts is another fruitful book for preaching texts. But there are sixty-six books in the "whole counsel of God." Our texts should be selected with the whole Bible before us. We are living in the New Testament dispensation, but that is no reason for neglecting the Old Testament as an inspired source for sermon texts. Paul used it. Peter used it. Stephen used it. Timothy did. They were all reasonably good preachers.

Sometimes a text is nothing but a pretext. You probably heard about the preacher who could preach baptism from any Bible text. Such use of the scripture is worse than a pretext. If we are faithful shepherds we will feed the flock on a good spiritual diet of a wide variety of Biblical subjects. Do not forget that a "hobby horse" in preaching is that type of preaching where you get off at the same place you got on.

2. *The Theme, subject or central thought.*

This is that portion of the sermon which is often referred to as the "idea" for the message. The terms theme and subject are used interchangeably to refer to this portion of the outline. The ideal method in securing a theme or subject is, after considering the needs of the congregations, to know God's Word so well as to be able to turn in it to that portion of scripture which would best fit the condition and so from this context select your text. From this find your idea, theme or subject. However, the method most often used is somewhat different. The preacher is conscious at all times of the needs of the flock. Rather than referring directly to God's Word for the theme, he finds it through one of many different means: Books, daily experiences, conversation, other ministers, etc. These contacts remind him of some Bible reference, or an idea which he hopes he can confirm with a Biblical reference or text. Both methods are used, the latter probably more frequently; but with a desire to develop a closer relationship of the preacher and his Bible, we will use the former method throughout our study.

Here are some qualities we should find in every theme employed by the man of God.

First of all, and most of all, the theme should be *clear. Nothing can be too clear.* It may be too common or too technical, but no subject can be too clear. Can you state your subject in one sentence? If you have difficulty in doing this you very likely are as yet not clear enough in your own mind to proceed in your next step of preparation. Just what do you hope to accomplish in your message? What is the idea as stated in a simple sentence?

If the subject does not "have" the preacher, the preacher will have a very difficult time "getting" the subject. The subject should be most absorbing to the minister. He should be intrigued, fascinated, entranced by the possibilities of his theme. The congregation is seldom as interested in a subject as the preacher, so if it is not of real interest to the man of God he can never make it of interest to those who hear.

There is a popular fault in the forming of a theme — it has to do with announcing one theme and then realizing that it is incomplete. The preacher tries to remedy the deficiency by adding another theme. He feels all he is doing is completing the subject, but actually he is confused in his own mind. His subject has not been defined, is incomplete. A good theme is complete in thought.

Let us make our themes or subjects forceful. If a subject is weak in its statement it is very likely to be weak in development. People are looking to the man of God for strength, for their inner needs. Let us give them a strong refuge from the Word of God. There is no room nor place for doubts or hesitation in the themes of the true preacher of the gospel.

Here are five themes selected from as many texts. From them select the ones that clearly develop the text and tell why. (Read the texts.)

(1) Heaven's Call. John 3:16.
(2) Life's Greatest Preparation. Amos 4:12.
(3) Your Inevitable Appointment. Heb. 9:27.
(4) Why be lost? Luke 13:3.
(5) What Christ could not do. Matt. 27:42.

Now *you* select the theme from the ones that have been mishandled. State it clearly in one brief statement.

Here are five more themes from one text. Tell which ones are interesting in their statement. Say why. Romans 12:1–2.

(1) How to be fashionable with God.
(2) Conformation and transformation.
(3) Paul's desire for the Roman saints.
(4) The constraint of God's mercies.
(5) Your spiritual service.

Point out which themes in this group are *not* complete in their statement; note:

(1) Romans 1:16 "I am not ashamed."
(2) Matt. 6:33 "What to seek."
(3) Matt. 13:45–46 "A Merchant's great discovery."
(4) Matt. 13:44 "God's acre of diamonds."
(5) Luke 15:11–24 "One sheep."

Why are the ones you selected incomplete? You restate them in a complete form.

Here is what I mean by forcefully stated themes: From the text I Cor. 13:1–6 we could select the theme of "love" but it can be stated in one of the two ways:

(1) "The Greatest Thing in the World" or
(2) "The Superiority of Love."

Which carries the most force in its statement? Why?

From the text of Heb. 11:1–2 we could select the theme of "faith" but it can be stated in one of the two ways:

(1) "The Inspired Definition of Faith" or
(2) "Heaven's Key to Success."

Which one contains the most force of statement? Why?

3. *The Introduction.*

The introduction is that portion of the sermon which introduces the theme from the text. To consider the introduction as the third step in the sermon outline is logical when considered chronologically, but it is not logical according to the actual preparation of the message. How can we possibly introduce a theme as it relates to the text and the message if we do not know the content and development of the sermon? So, although we consider it as third in the parts of the sermon, its actual preparation should be left until the body of the sermon has at least been outlined.

The characteristics of a good introduction.

Here is a text theme and introduction. I feel that it is a good introduction. Can you tell why?

Psa. 126:5–6.

"The Divine Formula for Soul Winning."

In Pittsburgh, Pennsylvania, in 1939 a million dollar building was finished. It was the new Post Office. Up the steps of this building went the first customer with a letter in his hand. In less than a moment the same man returned with the same letter in his hand. You see, they had built the Post Office and had completely equipped it for service, except that they had neglected to provide a slot for the mail.

This is a true story. But there is another true story that is even more absurdly tragic. It is to build a church and leave no method of soul winning. A church Jesus did promise to build, but we *do* have a *divine* formula. Here it is. Hear this text from God's book: Psa. 126:5–6.

Here is an introduction that is faulty. Tell me what is the matter with it.

Psa. 34:5.

"Radiant Religion."

Radiant religion is the religion of Jesus, not the religion of Mohammed or Zoroaster. These religions have nothing to offer in the realm of moral reform. But then moral reform is not the end of Christianity, either. Transformation and not reformation is the plea of the Master. So much of our religion is purely mundane and operates on the horizontal level. If we would lift up our faces to the horizon of redeeming grace we will be radiant. This is our discussion today — radiant religion.

A good introduction has the following characteristics:

1. It is a porch to the sermon; not a room in it. Therefore is does not *develop* the theme; it introduces it.

2. It serves the purpose of introducing the theme; therefore

it does not include more or less than the theme in its form, i.e. it is not broader than the theme or narrower.

3. It serves the purpose of attracting attention and interest. Hence its form will be such as to accomplish this end.

With these three characteristics in mind, evaluate your criticisms of the preceding introductions and determine whether your objections fall under one or more of these headings. If so, which? Write out the evaluation.

1. What is an explanation of a text? What is its purpose?

2. In what way should the preacher be able to say, "today hath this scripture been fulfilled in your ears"?

3. When is a text a pretext?

4. What is the ideal method of securing a theme for a sermon?

5. How can it be said that in the area of themes nothing can be too clear?

6. How do some preachers fail in an attempt to remedy an incomplete theme?

7. Why is it not logical to consider the introduction as third in point of development?

8. Give three characteristics of a good introduction.

Assignment Fifteen

Read the following discussion and answer the questions.

4. *The Proposition*

That portion of the message which states in one sentence the aim of the sermon.

This is the pivot of the entire sermon. The text, introduction and theme lead to it. The main and subdivisions develop it and the conclusion concludes it. Its importance, then, can hardly be over emphasized.

Here is a text: Matt. 25:1-12. From this text you select the theme. Maybe it will be "Foolish Virgins." What is the *aim* in your discussion of this subject? Surely you will have some definite purpose. What is it? Can you state it in one sentence? This is your proposition. Here are three possibilities:

(1) Characteristics of the foolish virgins.

(2) Reasons these virgins are called foolish.

(3) Lessons from the foolish virgins.

Here is a text, Gen. 22:1-14. The theme is "The Sacrifice of Abraham." Will you *formulate three possible propositions* for this theme? Say anything you want to about it, but say it in *one clear sentence.*

(1)

(2)

(3)

Here is another text. Gen. 28:10-22. The theme is "Jacob's Vision." Do the same as above.

(1)

(2)

(3)

Your statement of proposition must be clear, concise and complete. Remember: *Clear, concise, complete.*

One more try. Matt. 18:23-35. "The Unforgiving Servant." (All of these themes should be reworded for interesting statement).

Your propositions:

(1)

(2)

(3)

5. *The main divisions*

I am sure you could give me a definition of this portion of the outline. It is that portion of the outline which develops the proposition. It is but an enlargement of the proposition, a development of the aim stated in the proposition. Some have called them the unfolding of the theme. This they are, but only as the theme is unfolded through the proposition.

Here are some illustrations of what I mean:

Text: John 4:7-14.

"The Living Water."

"Some attributes of this living water."

Main divisions: I. It quenches thirst.

II. It becomes a spring within.

III. It is conditionally received.

Text: John 4:1–30.

"The Woman of Samaria" (This could be made to sound more interesting.)

"Some characteristics of this woman."

Main Divisions: I. She was a flagrant sinner.

II. She was an aroused questioner.

III. She was a bewildered trifler.

IV. She was an earnest listener.

V. She was a fearless testifier.

Text: I Cor. 6:2.

"Why be a Christian *now.*"

"Some reasons for being a Christian now."

Main Divisions: I. To keep sin from further cursing your body.

II. To place your influence on the side of God and right.

III. Because the Lord may come before morning.

IV. Because you may go into His presence tonight.

Now, here are some examples in which the main divisions are *not* right. Can you detect the difficulty? Write out your evaluations.

Text: John 2:13–19.

"The Cleansing of the Temple."

"Reasons for the cleansing."

Main Divisions: I. How the temple was defiled.

II. How the temple was cleansed.

III. The sign of authority as cleanser.

Text: John 6:30–40.

"The True Bread."

"Characteristics of the true bread."

Main Divisions: I. Came from heaven.

II. The way this bread is to be taken.

III. Results of eating this bread.

Text: Eph. 6:10–20.

"The Christian Armor."

"This armor and its uses."
Main Divisions: I. The enemy.
II. The warfare.
III. Praying and watching.

Good main divisions do not develop *more* than the proposition, *less* than the proposition nor *another* proposition. Which mistake was made in the above examples?

It is usually best to strive as much as at all possible to develop the main divisions right from the text as they are related to the theme and proposition.

6. *The subdivisions.*

It should be obvious by this time what we mean by subdivisions. Simply stated, they are those headings which serve to develop and enlarge the main divisions. The subdivisions stand in the same relationship to the main divisions that the main divisions do to the proposition.

Note: John 10:1–10.
"The Good Shepherd."
"Characteristics of the good shepherd."
I. He is Personal.
Subdivisions: 1. He knows each sheep by name.
2. He cares for each hurt of each sheep.
3. He finds pasture for each one.
II. He is Progressive.
You fill in the subdivisions. Find them in the text.

1.

2.

3.

III. He is Protective.

1.

2.

3.

What thoughts come to you as you attempt to develop the idea of a "Personal shepherd"? These thoughts become your subdivisions under the heading of "Personal Shepherd." What can you say that will develop the thought of a "progressive shepherd"? A "protective shepherd"? These, then, become your subdivisions.

What we have said of the main divisions we say of the subdivisions in development. There should be no overlapping in their development.

7. *The conclusion.*

This is a very important part of the outline and sermon. For this reason it should have definite form and purpose.

The appeal of the conclusion should be based squarely on the proposition and should not obtain its appeal from the last part of the last division.

It seems to me that there can be three definite parts to a conclusion: (1) a recapitulation of the leading thought of each main division, (2) a recapitulation of some of the personal applications made in the message, and (3) a direct appeal to the emotions with the intent of some definite action.

The purpose of a conclusion worthy of its name is to draw the force of the sermon together in such a manner as to carry an appeal to the conscience for a personal response to what has been preached.

Assignment Sixteen

Read the questions and answers. Here prepare
at least two questions of your own to ask in class.

A number of class questions that have been asked concerning the sermon outline:

1. "Do you have to have a text for every message?"

This has been answered before, but let us say again that there are some sermons that can be called "subject sermons." These would not require one specific Bible reference. Such subjects as: The Holy Spirit; The Word of God; The Christian; Prayer, etc.

Undoubtedly there will be references used in these sermons. It could be that some of them would carry a "starter text" but such subjects are so wide in their scope that they cannot be limited to one text.

2. "Does every sermon have to have clearly defined subdivisions?"

I assume that this question is asked with a desire to know

whether a sermon can be the most effective without subdivisions and not because the preacher is too lazy to work them out. I honestly feel that the development of the main divisions should be clearly defined — at least in the mind of the preacher. The working out of subdivisions accomplishes this end in the best way I know of.

3. "Will not this 'exacting' arrangement of your material become dry and dull?"

Some preachers can preach a dry, dull sermon on any subject on any occasion for the obvious reason that they themselves are dry and dull. The method of sermon building has very little to do with this lack. But if that same preacher had a clearly defined outline some of the precious souls who were interested in spite of his delivery would be able to follow and remember.

4. "Will not this method limit the work of the Holy Spirit?"

Here is a quotation from Harold Knott's book on How to Prepare a Sermon that very adequately answers this question: "Some have thought that it was limiting the work of the Holy Spirit to have a careful preparation of what one intends to say, not leaving the Divine Spirit free to express Himself. There can be no doubt about this theory being built upon a false foundation. To seek divine help in preparing the message is to depend upon the Spirit's guidance just as much as to wait till one is about to enter the pulpit and then call upon God. The world's greatest preachers have ever been those whose outlines reveal the most careful preparation" (p. 22).

Here are the facts.

May I ask you some very factual questions over the chapter we have just completed? Write out your answers and discuss them in class.

1. Could you draw a picture of a sermon outline? Try it.
2. When is a textual explanation needed?
3. How does the audience affect our choice of a text?
4. When is a text a pretext?
5. What is the suggested ideal method in finding a theme?
6. Name three qualities that should be found in every good theme.
7. What does the introduction introduce?
8. Name three characteristics of a good introduction.

9. Why is the proposition so important?
10. What is one popular mistake that is made in the forming of main divisions?
11. How does the text relate to the main divisions?
12. How are subdivisions and the proposition similar?
13. Give two attributes of good subdivisions.
14. Why is the conclusion important?
15. What are the three parts to the conclusion?

SUGGESTED READING

Blackwood, Andrew Watterson. *The Preparation of Sermons.* p. 125–151.

Jones, Bob, Jr. *How to Improve Your Preaching.* p. 32-46.

Jordan, G. Ray. *You Can Preach.* p. 101-113.

Chapter 4
How to Make a Sermon Outline

ONLY ONE LIFE

'Tis not for man to trifle. Life is brief,
    And sin is here.
Our age is but the falling of a leaf,
    A dropping tear.
We have no time to sport away the hours;
All must be earnest in a world like ours.

Not *many* lives, but only *one*, have we, —
    One, only one;
How sacred should that one life ever be,
    That narrow span!
Day after day filled up with blessed toil,
Hour after hour still bringing in new spoil.

HOW TO MAKE A SERMON OUTLINE

I believe we can offer to you a most helpful method in making an outline from any text in the Bible. We can show you a way that will enable you to formulate immediately a good, original, logical outline. This system of sermon outlining has been taught to hundreds of students for more than a decade. I believe you will be pleasantly surprised, if not thrilled, with the prospects for your preparation.

Assignment Seventeen

Before we can discuss the actual steps involved I would like your honest prayerful answer to the following questions:

1. Do you believe a sermon outline is essential to the most effective sermon? Tell why you answer as you do.

2. Do you believe the greatest preachers of the past used definite planning in their sermons? If you do or do not, specify at least three preachers to illustrate your answer.

3. Why is it that more preachers do not use sermon outlines or outlines in their sermons?

4. A sermon can become "a recitation instead of a revelation." Is an outline and its use ever at fault in this deficiency?

5. Could it be demonstrated that there was any preconceived plan in the sermons of Paul? If so, specify by example.

6. Do you honestly feel that you would be helped in the preparation of your sermons if you had a definite procedure to follow in formulating an outline? If so, specify just what help it would be to you.

7. Assuming that you feel the outline is an advantage, how detailed should it be to be effective?

Assignment Eighteen

Read the following discussion and do the exercise at the conclusion.

The Six Principles of Discussion.

All sermons are discussions. The forms of the sermons may vary, their purposes are many, their results are numerous, but *they are all discussions.* Here are *six principles of discussion:*

1. What?
2. Who?
3. Why?
4. When?
5. Where?
6. How?

As these six principles relate to a subject they discuss the subject in the following manner:

1. "What" discusses the characteristics or attributes of the subject. If the subject was "heaven" we would be noting its essential characteristics or qualities, such as:

    a. Heaven is *certain.*
    b. Heaven is *prepared.*
    c. Heaven is *near.*

2. "*Who*" discusses the "person or persons" involved in the subject. Again, if the subject was "heaven" we would note the persons involved, such as:

    a. Heaven and *the sinner.*
    b. Heaven and *the saint.*
    c. Heaven and *the Saviour.*

3. "*Why*" discusses the "reasons" involved in the subject. Of course you can give some real good reasons for heaven, such as:

    a. Because of *God's love.*
    b. Because of *man's need.*
    c. Because of *Christ's death.*

4. "*When*" discusses the "time" element. As in the subject of "heaven":

    a. *Yesterday* God prepared heaven.
    b. *Today* you can prepare for heaven.
    c. *Tomorrow* may be too late for heaven.

5. "*Where*" discusses the "position" of the subject. Note:

    a. Heaven is just on the other side of your heart's last beat.

    b. Heaven is where the saints have gone.

    c. Heaven is where Jesus is.

  6. "How" discusses "method or methods" of accomplishment. In the case of the subject at hand, we would want to know the method of obtaining heaven.

    a. By accepting the way to heaven.

    b. By walking in the way to heaven.

    c. By taking others with us.

Could we be so bold as to say that *all discussion* of *all subjects* is involved in these six principles? I ask this seriously. Are there *just* six things we can say about any subject? When we discuss:

  1. The "what" of it or its characteristics.

  2. The "who" of it or the persons involved.

  3. The "why" of it or its reasons.

  4. The "when" of it or the time element.

  5. The "where" of it or its position.

  6. The "how" of it or its method.

What have we left to discuss that has not been considered in these six principles?

It will be noted by those of special scrutiny that there is a certain overlapping in the use of the principles. For example, if we were to select a person as a subject of discussion, to talk about the "what" of this subject is also to obviously involve the principle of "who." There are other overlappings of principles, but this poses no difficulty in analysis inasmuch as the extension of the discussion determines which principle will receive the emphasis.

A thorough knowledge of these six principles of discussion is essential to the formulation of a good sermon outline. Learn them now if you do not already know them. What are they? Name them in any order, but name all six:

Fill in the Blanks.

  1. "What" discusses the —————————— of the subject.

  2. "Who" discusses the —————————— of the subject.

  3. "Why" discusses the —————————— of the subject.

  4. "When" discusses the —————————— of the subject.

  5. "Where" discusses the —————————— of the subject.

  6. "How" discusses the —————————— of the subject.

Assignment Nineteen

> Read this section carefully and answer the questions.

The Seven Steps to a Sermon Outline.

To obtain the seven parts to a sermon outline there are seven definite steps:

Step one: Obtain a text.

Find a text that appeals to you and in which you can see the answer to the needs of the congregation. Such a text might be Acts 17:30–31.

> "And the times of this ignorance God winked at; but now commandeth all men everywhere to repent: Because He hath appointed a day in which He will judge the world in righteousness by that man whom He hath ordained; whereof He hath given assurance unto all men, in that He hath raised him from the dead."

Step Two: From this text select *a theme.*

This theme is sometimes called "the idea" for the sermon. Make the central thought of the text your theme. Try your best prayerfully to evaluate the text and obtain the thought that is most clearly presented in the text. Such a theme from Acts 17:30–31 would be: "God's Judgment."

Step Three: Form a proposition for your theme by using one or more of the six principles of discussion.

Remember, we said there are *only six things* you can say about any subject. What are they? What is our subject? "God's Judgment." What is a proposition? A proposition is that portion of the outline which states in one sentence the aim of the message.

Do you want to discuss the "what" of God's Judgment? If you do, then your proposition would read: "Some of the characteristics of God's Judgment."

Do you wish to discuss the "who" of God's Judgment? Then your proposition would run: "Some of the persons involved in God's Judgment."

Perhaps you desire to discuss the "why" of God's Judgment. If so, your proposition would then read: "Some reasons for God's Judgment."

If you wanted to formulate a proposition employing the principle of "when," how would you fill in the following blank? "The ————————— for God's Judgment."

How would the proposition be worded if you used the principle of "where"? Of "how"?

If you want to use more than one of the six principles in the statement of the proposition, you may. In that case the proposition might appear as: "Some *reasons* and *persons* in God's Judgment; or using two others: "Some *methods* and *characteristics* in God's Judgment."

There is nothing to hinder you from using three or four principles if you wish. If you want to embrace all the principles in a general type of proposition, it can be done in the following manner: "Some truths concerning God's Judgment."

All principles are incorporated by the generic term *truths.* Or this one: "Some *facts* concerning God's Judgment."

This step may seem to some to be exceedingly obvious, but experience has demonstrated that the practice of it is anything but obvious.

Let us see. Suppose you take the "golden text" of the Bible, John 3:16, and select a theme from it and formulate a proposition for a message. Use the principle of "what" in your proposition.

Fill in the blanks:

Your text is John 3:16.

Your theme is: ⎯⎯⎯⎯⎯⎯⎯⎯⎯⎯⎯⎯⎯⎯⎯⎯

Your proposition reads: ⎯⎯⎯⎯⎯⎯⎯⎯⎯⎯⎯⎯⎯⎯

Now a proposition from the same text and then using the principle of "why":

Your theme is: ⎯⎯⎯⎯⎯⎯⎯⎯⎯⎯⎯⎯⎯⎯⎯⎯

Your proposition reads: ⎯⎯⎯⎯⎯⎯⎯⎯⎯⎯⎯⎯⎯⎯

Step Four: Construct your main divisions through a development of your proposition.

Remember our text and theme?

Text: Acts 17:30-31.

Theme: "God's Judgment."

We suggested a number of possible propositions for this theme. Let us use this one:

Proposition: "Some reasons for God's Judgment."

How many reasons shall we use? There is no way to determine the number other than your own desire in developing the subject.

Can you think of three reasons for Jehovah's judgment? If you can, you have three headings for your main divisions of your message. If you can only think of two, then use them. You will have a two division sermon. Or it may be you have thought of more than three. Just what are the reasons for God's Judgment?

I. Because
II. Because
III. Because

Each of these forms a heading for your main division of your sermon.

Supposing your proposition read: "Some persons involved in God's Judgment." How would your main divisions appear? Work up three of them in as many words:

I.
II.
III.

If you said in your proposition: "Some characteristics of God's Judgment," what would be the wording of your main divisions? Are the following correct?

I. It is certain.
II. God will judge through Christ.
III. Because of unpunished sin.

If they are correct, explain why. If not, explain why not.

Some of the principles have certain prefixes that appear in their development. Such prefixes are:

a. "Because" for *why.*
b. "By" for *how.*

Step Five: Obtain your subdivisions through a direct development of your main divisions.

The question in this step is "How shall we obtain the subdivisions?" Here is the answer:

"Allow the statement of the main division to act as a theme. Apply one or more of the six principles of discussion to it. This will form a sub-proposition; the development from this sub-proposition will be the headings of your subdivisions."

Note: If our main division is:

I. The certainty of God's Judgment.

There are only six things we can say about the certainty of

God's Judgment. Which of the six shall it be? Suppose we use
"why." How would the sub-proposition read?
    I. The certainty of God's Judgment.
Sub-proposition: *Reasons for the certainty of God's judgment.*
The answers to the sub-proposition will be the headings of your
subdivisions, such as:
    1. Because man's sin demands it.
    2. Because God's Word states it.
    3. Because Jesus was raised to be our Judge.
Supposing the heading of our main division was:
    I. The Judge of the judgment.
What would be the first step in obtaining the subdivision?
Assuming you use the principle of "what" in forming your sub-
proposition, how would it read? Fill in the blanks:

_____

From this sub-proposition form your subdivisions, such as:
    1.
    2.
    3.
There is one other way to form subdivisions. If our main
heading was:
    I. The Issues of the Judgment.
You can use the statement of the six principles as subdivisions,
such as:
    1. Characteristics of these issues.
    2. Reasons for these issues.
    3. Methods of revealing these issues.
The above method is simply using three sub-propositions as
subdivisions. Try forming subdivisions for this main division
using *both* methods.
    I. The Books of the Judgment.
Sub-proposition:
Subdivisions:
    1.
    2.
    3.
Step Six: Develop your subdivisions using the principles of
"reprove, rebuke and exhort." Cf. II Tim. 4:1-3.

More of this method of developing the sermon will appear in chapter five. Suffice it to say here that it is our persuasion that this is the divine formula for the development of the subdivisions.

Step Seven: Construct a conclusion based upon the proposition. We are to devote a whole chapter to this portion of the outline. There are three definite parts to an effective conclusion:

1. A recapitulation of the force of the main divisions.
2. A recapitulation of the force of some of the personal applications made in the sermon.
3. A direct appeal to the emotions with intention of persuasion.

The formation of the introduction is usually left until the last step, for it is always easier to form it after we know what to introduce.

SUGGESTED READING

Garrison, Webb B. *The Preacher and His Audience.* p. 150–170.

Pattison, Harwood T. *The Making of the Sermon.* p. 51–94.

Sanders, Norred Tant Cogdill. *Preaching in the Twentieth Century.* p. 29–39.

Chapter 5

The Development of the Sermon

FOR OTHERS

Lord, help me live from day to day
In such a self-forgetful way
That even when I kneel to pray
    My prayer shall be for *others*.

Help me in all the work I do
To ever be sincere and true,
And know that all I'd do for you
    Must needs be done for *others*.

Let Self be crucified and slain,
And buried deep; and all in vain
May efforts be to rise again
    Unless to live for *others*.

And when my work on earth is done,
And my new work in heaven's begun,
May I forget the crown I've won
    While thinking still of *others*.

Others, Lord, yes, others,
    Let this my motto be:
Help me to live for others,
    That I may live like thee.

THE DEVELOPMENT OF THE SERMON

Assignment Twenty

Read the following discussion and answer the questions.

If we were to select a text for this chapter it would be that text of all texts for the gospel preacher, II Tim. 4:1–2.

"I charge thee in the sight of God, and of Christ Jesus, who shall judge the living and the dead, and by His appearing and His kingdom: PREACH THE WORD; be *urgent* in season, out of season; *reprove, rebuke, exhort,* with all longsuffering and teaching."

How many times have you heard this scripture read? How often have you heard preachers exhorted to follow it? No reading or exhortation on this point is resisted by the true man of God. Above and beyond everything else in life as a preacher we should indeed "Preach the Word."

But is it being done? Are we obeying this divine injunction? We cannot say we are just because we assent to the fact that it should be done, or because someone exhorts us to do so. Is it enough to have some vaguely defined ideal as our purpose in preaching?

To all these questions I am sure you will answer in the negative. I am also persuaded that if we today were preaching the Word like Paul exhorted Timothy to preach the Word we would have at least somewhat the same results. The results that were had by Timothy, Titus, Paul, Barnabas and others as they preached the Word are not the results that some of us have today.

But there is an answer to this very real problem. It is found in the text: "Preach the Word"...yes, but *how* shall we preach the Word? Note the divine formula for preaching:

"...*be urgent* in season, out of season; *reprove, rebuke, exhort...*"

All sermons should contain these elements in their development. The subjects may be as varied as the wide range of Biblical texts but all can and should contain these divine essentials. It might be well to clearly define these terms:

1. *"Reprove."* This is not a synonym for "chide." As it is used here it means "to bring to proof." It carries the thought of presenting evidence for demonstration. We might say that a subject not only ought to be proved but *"re-proved."*

2. *"Rebuke."* "To reprimand, chasten, or chide." To "rebuke" in the divine sense is to bring us face to face with our sins and shortcomings. The concern felt in our heart is the "rebuke" of God through His Word.

3. *"Exhort."* "To incite by appeal or argument to good deeds." This is the action word. After the facts have been presented and conviction has been established, then a call to action is in order.

A wonderful example of the use of these three elements in preaching is seen in the sermon of Peter on the day of Pentecost. (Acts 2:14–37).

1. "Reprove." Peter demonstrated or proved in a wonderful array of evidence that Jesus was the Christ. "A man approved of God unto you by mighty works and wonders and signs which God did by Him in the midst of you, even as ye yourselves know" (Acts 2:22).

2. "Rebuke." He brought the deepest type of conviction through the accusation that they had crucified the Messiah. "...ye by the hands of lawless men did crucify and slay..." "Let all the house of Israel therefore know assuredly that God hath made Him both Lord and Christ, this Jesus whom ye crucified" (Acts 2:23, 36).

3. "Exhort." "With many other words He *testified* [a word that would include both reprove and rebuke] and *exhorted* them saying, Save yourselves from this crooked generation" (Acts 2:40).

It is because we have not used this divine order in preaching that we have failed to have a better response.

Here are some candid questions; give them an honest answer.

1. Is it really possible to "be *urgent"* in season and out of season? If not, why not? If so, how?

2. Name three occasions when you would consider it "out of season" for being urgent in preaching.

3. Do you feel that it is true that we are not having in our preaching the results that were had in apostolic times? If so, specify two differences.

4. What is meant by "reprove" as used in II Tim. 4:2? If something is proved, what is the purpose in "re-proving" it?

5. Do you feel that it is ethical to "rebuke" another fellow creature? Doesn't this enter the field of judging? (Cf. Matt. 7:1).

6. If we are to incite to action, what must be appealed to in the nature of man? We are saying here that it is not enough to appeal only to the intellect — what else must be touched?

Assignment Twenty-one

Read the following discussion and write out the exercises.

Let us take our example outline as it appeared in chapter four and see how this formula of development works out in experiment.

Text: Acts 17:30–31.

Theme: "God's Judgment" (This need not be the title of the sermon.)

Proposition: "Some reasons for God's Judgment."

I. Because of man's sin.

Sub-proposition: Some characteristics of man's sin that calls forth God's judgment.

1. Wilfulness.

How is the thought of wilful sin going to be developed?

   a. Prove it! (reprove)

   b. Apply it! (rebuke)

   c. Call for action! (exhort)

It is important to note that all thoughts do not need the same amount of demonstration. Does the wilfulness of man's sin need demonstration? This is answered solely by the need of the audience to whom we speak. For the sake of example, let us say that this point *does* need proving and "re-proving." How shall this be done? Alan H. Monroe in his book, *Principles and Types of Speech,* p. 221, gives seven forms of verbal support:

1. Explanation.

2. Analogy or comparison.
3. Illustration (detailed example).
   a. Hypothetical illustration.
   b. Factual illustration.
4. Specific instances (undeveloped examples).
5. Statistics.
6. Testimony.
7. Restatement.

Shall we notice how these seven forms could be used in the "reproving" of "how wilful sin calls forth God's judgment?"

1. *Explanation.* There is no need to give here any detailed development of the subject. All that is needed in this type of proof is a simple exposition of the subject. Something like this would suffice:

> If God is a righteous judge, and we know He is, then sin cannot go unpunished. The punishment of sin must follow wilful sin or God's perfect spiritual economy is destroyed. As a father who loves his children is expressing his love in discipline, so is God's love expressed, and unavoidably so, against the wilful sin of man.

2. *Analogy or Comparison.* The analogy was briefly used in the above explanation. Here is an example that could serve to establish the thought:

> We can control the decisions of eternity, but we cannot control the results. Have you ever watched the mixture of two chemicals? While the chemicals remain separate they are but dry powder; put them together and there could be an explosion. After the chemicals are mixed there is *nothing* we can do to alter the result. So it is with the higher laws of God. When we mix wilful sin in the conduct of our life, we cannot alter or hinder the judgment of God. As immutable as the law of gravity is the judgment of God, upon wilful sin. More certain than the rising of the sun in the canopy of space is the rising of the son of righteousness to the throne of judgment to deal with every transgression.

3. *Illustration (detailed example).*

We are all acquainted with the most popular of all types of proof — a story to illustrate the point. Here are two or three of them as examples:

a. Hypothetical. (It should be in order here to say that we

know that an illustration does not offer further proof, but it does serve to enforce the point already made.)

"Suppose someone were to offer me a thousand dollars for every soul that I might earnestly try to lead to Christ. Would I endeavor to lead any more souls to Him than I am endeavoring to do now? Is it possible that I would attempt to do *for money*, even at the risk of blunders or ridicule, what I hesitate or shrink from doing now in obedience to God's command? Is my love of money stronger than my love of God or souls? What is *your* reply to this solemn, searching question?

"Suppose I were to see a blind man unknowingly approaching the brink of a high precipice and that I were to sit by without concern or any effort to warn or save him from certain death, would I not be as guilty of his death in God's sight as though I had murdered him outright? The death of the body which might have been (but was not) prevented is a terrible thing; but how about the preventable death of a human soul — perchance of many souls — for which God may hold me responsible?"

—From the book *"Soul Winning"* by George B. Thompson, pages 52, 53, 54.

b. Factual.

"He who rules his spirit is the greatest of all conquerors. Alexander conquered the world, but was not able to conquer himself and died in a drunken debauch. Napoleon waded through seas of blood to gratify an unholy ambition. For a time he was worshiped as a hero, but at last experienced the instability of earthly honor and died in exile.

"Louis XVI came to the throne of France shortly before the French Revolution and although the country was greatly embarrassed financially, his court was filled with beauty and splendor. He flourished for a time, but his fame did not endure. In a little while those who had lauded him were calling for his life. His proud wife, the beautiful Marie Antoinette, rode to her execution bound in a cart and seated on a coffin which in a few minutes was to hold her dead body.

"In the middle of the eleventh century there was a Mohammedan prince named Saladin. Ascending the throne of the ancient Pharaohs and guiding the Moslem armies, he rolled back the tide of European invasion. The wealth of the Orient was in his lap; the fate of millions hung upon his lips. But at last death, the common conqueror of all, came to smite the crown from his brow and dash the scepter from his hand. As he lay upon his deathbed, looking back upon visions of earthly glory and forward to the future, his soul was overwhelmed with emotion.

"Rousing himself from his reverie, the sultan said, 'Prepare and bring me my winding sheet.' It was brought and unfolded before him and he gazed upon it long and earnestly. At last he said, 'Bring here the banner around which my chosen guards have rallied in my victories.' It was brought and in silence the attendants awaited his further directions. He paused a moment, then said, 'Remove those silken folds and attach to the staff this winding sheet.' It was done. As the dimmed eye of the dying man rested upon the emblem of mortality while it hung on the staff around which he had rallied his legions on the field of blood, he commanded, 'Let the crier, accompanied by musicians playing a funeral dirge, pass through all the streets of the city and at every corner wave the banner and proclaim, 'This is all that remains of Saladin's glory and power.' " (*Ibid.,* pages 148, 149–150).

The inevitable judgment of God upon the wilful sin of man is so very graphically pointed out in these two stories. There are innumerable such stories written and unwritten. If you do not know where to get such illustrations, start by obtaining two or three books of illustrations. The Bible should be the first source book, then those illustration books that contain *stories that have been proven by use.*

4. *Specific Instances* (undeveloped examples).

It would not be difficult to develop this form from the scriptures. Note:

a. The imagination of man's heart was evil continually. (cf. Gen. 6:5). As a high mountain calls for the clouds and thunder, so the clouds of God's disapproval and the thunder of His judgment is called forth by man's wilful sin.

b. "And the men of Sodom were sinners before God" (cf. Gen. 13:13). The sons-in-law of Lot thought him to be mad. But their disbelief and ridicule did not stay the fire and brimstone of God's judgment upon wilful sin.

c. Two shallow graves dug in haste and fear testified to those of the church in Jerusalem that hypocrisy would not go unpunished. (cf. Acts 5:1–5).

There could be many more specific instances produced to illustrate this form. Suffice it to say that the terse descriptive phrase is what is needed here.

5. *Statistics.*

What statistics could be produced that would prove that wilful sin cannot go unpunished? Perhaps you could search out such information:

a. How many died in the fields of Bethshemesh because of wilful sin?

b. How many priests or other servants of God have paid with their life for wilful sin? (Look them up; there are several.)

c. How many cities have been destroyed for wilful sin?

d. How much gold and silver has been lost because of such sin?

e. How much property forfeited?

These five items given in rapid succession would make an impression.

6. *Testimony.*

In preaching no testimony could be better than the word of God. When we think of testimony we usually associate it with a person. Those persons mentioned in God's Word can be brought forward to testify on many subjects. The subject before us is a good one.

a. Suppose we were (hypothetically) to call upon someone to testify concerning the action of Nadab and Abihu (Exo. 10:1-2) that brought the judgment of God upon them. How would the expression of this one read? Select another Levite for a specific person. How would he describe the action of these two sons of Aaron and God's judgment upon their wilful sin? Write up a short paragraph expressing in the first person such a testimony.

b. Samson is in the prison house of the Philistines. He is shorn not only of his hair, but of his strength with God and man. As he pushes the millstone he is meditating upon the sure judgment of God upon his wilful sin. What would he say in his soliloquy? You express it, but make it as carefully accurate as possible.

c. What of the testimony of David and his sin with Bathsheba? Read Psalms 51 for an expression of his heart on the subject. Read also the historical account of the sin and then formulate in the first person a word from David upon the judgment of God on wilful sin.

    d. You could do the same with Saul of Tarsus, Judas, etc.

    7. *Restatement.*

This form could only be used when one or more of the others has been employed. When restating anything, be especially careful to change the words but not to change the thought. Monotony is but a result of a lack of enthusiastic interest on the part of the preacher. You can restate the development of wilful sin and not be burdensome at all if you want to, and I mean *really* want to.

These seven forms of verbal support should all be used in the first step in developing your message. Let us see if we can recall them from memory. They were:

1. ———————————————

2. ——————————— or ———————————

3. ————————————— (————— ——————)

    a. ——————————— ———————————

    b. ——————————— ———————————

4. ————— ——————(————— ——————)

5. ———————————————

6. ———————————————

7. ———————————————

Now is the time to make these methods of development yours. If you were unable to fill in the above blanks work on it until you can, "not somehow but triumphantly."

Here is a little exercise for application of what you have learned: Suppose your point of proof and reproof was: "God rewards righteousness." Reprove this in the following three ways:

    1. By analogy and comparison.

    2. By specific instances.

    3. By statistics.

Assignment Twenty-two
Read carefully and write out the exercises.

We now come to the second portion of the development of the sermon. How shall we *apply* the message? "Reprove, *rebuke,* exhort with all long suffering and teaching." The total message should be applicable. We will use our example outline. To refresh our memories we will reproduce it in its entirety:

Text: Acts 17:30–31.
Theme: "God's Judgment."
Proposition: "Some reasons for God's judgment."
I. Because of man's sin.
Sub-proposition: Some characteristics of man's sin that calls forth God's judgment.
1. Wilfulness.

Let us assume that this has been proved and reproved by one or more of the seven ways suggested. This effort will not have exceeded two or three minutes time in the preaching — possibly less. You are now ready to *apply* the truth to life. How shall it be accomplished? It is well to remember that man lives in two realms:

1. *Social.* In his contact with his fellow man.
2. *Spiritual.* His relationship with God.

This being true *all* application of truth will fall under one or the other of these relationships.

What are the Christian responsibilities of man's social life? This question has tremendous implications. Indeed, the entire Way of life as outlined by our Lord is involved. It is good constantly to keep before our hearts some of the outstanding truths He gave in this area:

(1) Kindness   (2) Generosity   (3) Courage   (4) Patience
        (5) Meekness   (6) Self-control   (7) Love
                                              a. for friends
                                              b. for enemies
        (8) Cheerfulness   (9) Steadfastness   (10) Joy

Where will wilful sin find its application in the social life? Will it be in the matter of showing *kindness,* or *courage,* or *patience?* As an application of *generosity* will it be in giving when there is no possibility of return to us by the one to whom we have given? Could we point out the need for *courage* in our daily life? Ah, how we could all do with this quality in so many ways. It should be plain by now that any one of the above questions is fruitful of development.

Enter into this matter for yourself. Name three principles Jesus taught in our association one with another that we have *not* listed:

1. ————————————————

2. ————————————————

3. ————————————————

Just a word about the manner of development in this area. Be positive, firm, but kindly in your rebuke, "looking to yourself lest you also be tempted."

Suppose we follow out the development of the subdivision we have for an example:

1. Wilful sin brings God's judgment.
   a. Prove it.
      (1) By testimony or
      (2) By statistics, or
      (3) By any one or more of the other forms we suggested.
   b. Apply it.
      (1) *In the social life of man.* This could be developed in the area of the lack of: Kindness, patience, self-control, etc. Give some definite scriptural development on this. We can never "rebuke" another fellow creature with human authority. We want to feel that *God* is speaking to our hearts. That "it is God that worketh in us both to will and to work His good pleasure" (Cf. Phil 2:11). How easy it should be to show how we sin wilfully in the lack of patience.

It might be well to point out that the seven forms of verbal support can be used in the development of the application.

      (2) What about application in the *spiritual realm of living?* It is actually impossible to separate these two realms. We have arbitrarily separated them so as to better enable us to develop the thought. In our

social life we are answerable to God, but we are thinking now of our personal relationship to God in a way in which other persons are only indirectly associated. I mean in the area of: (a) Prayer; (b) Bible study; (c) Attendance of services; (d) Testimony to others; (e) Remaining conscious of His presence.

How do we wilfully sin in the above mentioned ways? We ask the question to call forth some type of answer. Ah, how short we are in this.

Let me hasten to say here that our development of rebuke *must* be great in variety both of content and development. Nothing will dull the hearing and turn the heart against reproof like "nagging."

If your thought to be demonstrated and applied was: *The study of the Word of God,* how would you go about applying it? Supposing it had already been proven and you were prepared to apply it. How would you go about it? In the examples below, which one is the best?

1. The study of the Word of God.
   a. Proved and "reproved" by analogy or comparison.
   b. It is to be applied to the social life of man.
      (1) The lack of kindness can be traced to a lack of the study of the Word of God.
      (2) We would all have more patience and joy if we studied the Word of God more.
      (3) What a greater love we would have for one another and for our enemies if we studied the Bible more.

Under each of the above stated points development could be made from one or more of the seven forms of verbal support.

2. The study of the Word of God.
   a. Proved and "reproved" by analogy or comparison.
   b. It is to be applied to the spiritual life of man.
      (1) How can we pray to God and talk with Him when we fail to allow Him to speak to us through His Word?
      (2) How can we effectively speak to others if we have failed to allow God to speak His message to our hearts?

> (3) What will develop a consciousness of God's omnip-
> otence and its relationship to us better than a daily
> study of His Word?
> Fill in the blanks:
> 1. I chose the first example because: ——————————

———————————————————————————————————

> 2. I chose the second example because: ——————————

———————————————————————————————————

Now, will you make up your own development in the area of "rebuke" on this thought?

The need for hospitality among Christians.

Assignment Twenty-three

Read carefully the following discussion and write out the exercise.

We come now to the third and final portion in the development of a sermon. After we have demonstrated the truth and applied it, how shall we secure action? "Reprove, rebuke, *exhort* with all longsuffering and teaching." Of all three, this is the most important and the most difficult of development.

Once again we are indebted to Allan H. Monroe for this list of what he calls "types of motive appeals" (*Principles and Types of Speech,* page 196). Note them carefully, for these are the motives to which you must appeal (in a religious application) to secure action from your audience:

1. Acquisition and saving.	10. Independence.
2. Adventure.	11. Loyalty.
3. Companionship.	12. Personal enjoyment.
4. Creating.	13. Power and authority.
5. Curiosity.	14. Pride.
6. Destruction.	15. Reverence or worship.
7. Fear.	16. Revulsion.
8. Fighting.	17. Sex attraction.
9. Imitation.	18. Sympathy.

Some of the above motives do not lend themselves as well as others for our use, but they are all present in the hearts of those to whom we speak. There is a core of truth in each of these which we can use when appealing for action. Note:

1. *Acquisition and saving.*

Surely self-preservation is one of the most basic of human desires. This thought immediately calls to mind the saving of the soul. This is one of the underlying of all appeals for action, but there are many other things in our natures that are in need of saving that the soul might ultimately be saved. I refer to those virtues that have lapsed or those sins from which we need to be saved. Let us obtain a clear picture of the need of man in these regards and use this motive of appeal in our exhortation or call for action.

2. *Adventure.*

This is one motive for action that is sadly neglected in preaching—and yet it should not be so. There is nothing so filled with adventure as an experience with God if we have it in our heart to make it so. But if you do not feel the thrill of the Christian experience, how can you use this as a real basis of action for others? May our hearts be warmed on this truth. At any rate, you can see how such a motive could be appealed to in calling for action.

3. *Companionship.*

Is not this what Jesus promised when He said, "Come, follow me"? Not only commitment to Him, but companionship with Him. The fellowship of Christ and God and fellow Christians ought to be emphasized in calling for action. It should be apparent by this time that not every one of these can be used with every subject, but to many subjects many of them can be used. With a little "sanctified imagination" and common sense their application is obvious.

4. *Creating.*

This is part of the "image of God" that we should want to create. All of us are builders, but how are we building? In what are you investing your life? These are the questions that relate to the application of this motive. What an unsurpassed area for creating in the kingdom of God. Come and build for eternity.

> "Only one life, t'will soon be past
>   Only what is done for Christ will last."
> "The moving finger writes,
>   And having writ, moves on;
>   Not all your piety, nor wit,
> Shall lure it back to cancel half a line;
> Nor all your tears wipe out a word of it."

What will it be that you have created while on this earth?

5. *Curiosity.*

Man has a natural desire for investigation. This is a healthy concern. We ought to capitalize on it for Christ and make the Christian religion so interesting that we will arouse a personal desire to investigate. There is so much to know and make ours. This impression should be passed on to those who are hearing.

Let me break into the stream of thought with a question that should be answered before we proceed. By this time I believe I can hear some of you saying to yourself, "How will it *ever* be possible to include *so much* under each subdivision and still confine the sermon to thirty minutes or less in length?"

This is a good question and one that is natural when you are confronted with all the material that we have been placing before you to be used under the development of subdivisions. Let me give a concise yet complete answer to this question. In the first place, let me say that it *is* possible to include all three points of development under *each* main division and still hold within reasonable time limits. What I mean is that you can "reprove, rebuke and exhort" under each subdivision and still let the folk out by "twelve o'clock." This can be done providing we know just *what* we are going to say and just *how* we are going to say it. If you had a two division sermon with two subdivisions under each main division you could use three minutes in the development of each and every subdivision and yet have three minutes for the introduction and five minutes for the conclusion and still only preach for twenty minutes. If you had three divisions with two subdivisions under each main division you could use the same ratio and only preach for twenty-six or twenty-seven minutes.

Our difficulty is that we do not know just exactly what we want to say, much less just how we want to say it; therefore it takes a long time to say a little. But let me hasten to add that *all* sermons need not and should not be developed in the same manner. Every subdivision does not need to be "proved and reproved." Some facts are self-evident and we want to use the time on "rebuke" or "exhort." Once again, some truths are not only self-evident in their thought, but also in their application. Therefore the whole time will be profitably spent in calling for action on the truth.

There is really only one rule that infallibly applies in development: *The three divine elements of reprove, rebuke and exhort should be found somewhere in the development of every sermon. The audience and the subject will determine where.*

6. *Destruction.*

There seems to be within man a desire to destroy as well as build. When this desire is applied to that which is evil, it is good and accomplishes good. We need to challenge people to know that they are either building for Christ or "fighting against" Him. As the Master has said: "He that is not for me is against me." Come join in the battle against sin, not righteousness. This thought of enlisting the desire to destroy on the right side is a good one and should and could be used much more than it is.

7. *Fear.*

This is a very real motive. The fear of eternal destruction should ever be uppermost in the mind and soul of the preacher of the good news. After all it is good news about what? "That Christ died to *save* sinners." To save them from what? From Hell. If we do not believe that a man is surely and eternally lost we will not preach like God would have us do. All men are afraid of something. Let them know whom to "fear" and why. This motive must not be neglected. "The fear of the Lord is the *beginning* of knowledge."

8. *Fighting.*

This follows close in the area of destruction. This is the spirit of competition that can be very healthy in its spiritual use. The thought to appeal to for the man outside of Christ is to come into the fellowship where there is a real purpose to competition. We are talking about fair competition in the area of seeing just how much we can do for the Lord in comparison to anyone else. Not for the praise of men, but for the praise of the Lord. But none the less the spirit of competition is always present and we had as well use it than to ignore it. Let us each count others better than himself and realize that after we have done all we are unprofitable servants, but still *do all we can* in this competitive world; and I believe God would have it so and made it so.

9. *Imitation.*

A whole treatise could be written of "An Imitation of Christ and its Great Desirability." Indeed, many treatises have been written. Man is strongly drawn with a desire to imitate someone. Why not appeal to an imitation of the perfect, the highest, the best. Our call in this motive should be to more than an imitation, but to a participation in Christ. What a wonderfully worthwhile thing it is to ask men not only to be reconciled to God, but to be like God, as He is portrayed in Jesus. Such call should be in the definite. We should ask men to be like Jesus in some definite way; in some personal virtue; in some plain characteristic.

> I have listed half of the motive appeals to be used in exhortation. Now you list and develop the other nine. Here is the list with a brief explanation. You enlarge upon it much in the way that I have for the first group.

10. *Independence.*

Appeal to the "dignity of man"; i.e., that he is an individual and is important and meaningful in the eyes of God. This he could not find in the world. You enlarge and apply this point as well as the rest of them.

11. *Loyalty.*

To whom are you loyal? You are loyal to someone. Is it to God or Satan?

12. *Personal enjoyment.*

In Christ we are promised "joy"; the permanent type of enjoyment. In the world we have "pleasure" only passing and unsatisfying.

13. *Power and authority.*

We can have power — wonderful power that we can have no other place. It is the power of the gospel. We are using something of the greatest power. Our power and authority is lost in the power and authority of God.

14. *Pride.*

This of course must never be applied to the pride of self. Indeed, that would be the very opposite of the teaching of Jesus. But there is a certain sense of the "peace that passeth understanding" in accepting and following Jesus. We are glad we did and are glad to say so. We approve what we have done because God approves it.

15. *Reverence or worship.*

"Man is incurably religious" someone has said. Make your reverence and worship mean something. Direct it toward the right one in the right way.

16. *Revulsion.*

If man is to be repelled by some things (and he is), then let us "abhor evil."

17. *Sex attraction.*

In Christ we can learn the right and holy relationship that can and should exist between sexes.

18. *Sympathy.*

Appeal to the sympathy of man as well as his use of sympathy.

Assignment Twenty-four

> Here is a sermon outline containing the development through the first division. Your task is to write out word for word the development of the two subdivisions employing "reprove, rebuke and exhort." After you have finished, read it out loud in class with emphasis. Time yourself.

Text: Matthew 27:22: "Pilate saith unto them, What then shall I do unto Jesus who is called Christ?"

Theme: "What Shall I Do With Jesus" (Could also be the title).

Proposition: A consideration of the answers of some *persons* to this question.

I. The answer of Pilate: "I will evade Him."
Sub-proposition: Characteristics of Pilate's answer.

  1. Illogical. He could not do it.
    a. Reprove.
    b. Rebuke (Remember the divine injunction "be urgent.")
    c. Exhort.
  2. Amounted to rejection.
    a. Reprove.
    b. Rebuke (Remember the divine injunction "be urgent.")
    c. Exhort.

II. The answer of Martha cf. Luke 10:38–42 "I will neglect Him."
Sub-proposition: Characteristics of Martha's answer.
   1. Came from a 'good woman.'
     a. Reprove.
     b. Rebuke.
     c. Exhort.
   2. Amounted to rejection.
     a. Reprove.
     b. Rebuke.
     c. Exhort.

SUGGESTED READING.

Gibbs, Alfred. *The Preacher and His Preaching.* p. 267–286.
Knott, H. H. *How to Prepare a Sermon.* p. 98–114.
Luccock, Halford E. *In the Minister's Workshop.* p. 148–163.

Chapter 6

The Delivery of the Sermon

THE BEST

Christ wants the best. He in the far-off ages
    Once claimed the firstlings of the flock, the
        finest of the wheat;
And still he asks his own with gentlest pleading
    To lay their highest hopes and brightest
        talents at his feet.
He'll not forget the feeblest service, humblest love,
He only asks that from our store we give to him
    The best we have.

Christ gives the best. He takes the hearts we offer,
    And fills them with his glorious beauty, joy,
        and peace;
And in his service as we're growing stronger,
    The calls to grand achievement still increase.
The richest gifts for us on earth, or in the
    heaven above,
Are hid with Christ in God. In Jesus we receive
    The best we have.

And is our best too much? O friends, let us remember
    How once our Lord poured out his soul for us
And in the prime of his mysterious manhood
    Gave up his precious life upon the cross!
The Lord of lords, by whom the worlds were made,
Through bitter grief and tears gave us
    The best he had.

THE DELIVERY OF THE SERMON

Assignment Twenty-five

Read this discussion prayerfully and answer the eleven questions.

Up to this moment the sermon is dead! Oh, it may live in your heart and mind, but it is unborn to the person for whom it was prepared. It is only in the delivery of the sermon that it becomes a living thing — and a sermon should live. Each message should live of itself. Each sermon has a particular point to it; a particular object as well as subject. But this it can never have until it is properly delivered. We could never overemphasize the importance of a good delivery. Do you really desire with all your heart to have a truly effective delivery for your sermons? Then answer these questions with a complete abandon of self.

1. Do you really believe that the average listener is "sitting on the edge of his seat" waiting to hear you?

2. Is it not true that the average listener is much more interested in himself and his interests than he is in you even if you are the preacher?

This being so, if you do not captivate his interest and attention hadn't you and he both just as well stayed home?

3. Even if you believe the listener *must* be stimulated to become a real participant, is it not true that if you do not say what you have to say *in the right manner* you will not have either his interest or his attention?

4. This being true, are you ready honestly and personally to conclude that the *one* most important factor in your preaching is the delivery?

5. See if you can sincerely agree with this conclusion: I have read at least twenty-five books on the subject of homiletics and several more on the matter of delivery, but I have yet to find

a set of rules that are of real value in the realm of delivery. Rules are for those who have something to deliver, not for those who have not. Persons are so varied in their innate abilities and modes of expression that the only rule I can apply to everyone is *"Be urgent."* After one has learned to be urgent then it is well enough to point out the best use of urgency. But without that divine requisite all rules fall to the ground. This is important. Do you accept this conclusion?

You need not express your urgency with the same mannerisms that I use or someone else uses; but if men are to hear and heed your message *it must be delivered in urgency.* The type of urgency will vary with the subject of the message, but the same heaven sent drive will be there — "urgency." Do you believe this?

6. Why are you not more urgent in your preaching? Not — why is not your preacher or your teacher or your friend more urgent. But honestly now, list three reasons why *you* are not more urgent. What is it that kills or quenches urgency?

1. ———————————————————————

2. ———————————————————————

3. ———————————————————————

7. Do you really believe it is possible for all men to be urgent? You know some persons, I am sure, who never seem to get excited about anything. How could they be expected to be urgent?

8. List three things you feel would really help to develop your urgency. Make them specific:

1. ———————————————————————

2. ———————————————————————

3. ———————————————————————

9. Were you ever in an automobile accident, a fire or some other type of emotional crisis? If so, *when* was it that you could describe this incident with the most reality? Was it not just shortly after it happened? Were you not then able (or even now) to close your eyes and live over again in your memory and imagination the reality of what happened to you and to tell it with reality?

If this is true, and I know it is, is not urgency very directly connected with reality? In other words, you can only make real to your audience what is real to you. *Urgency* then becomes an essential accompanying quality to *reality*. Of course if you do not care to relive the experience either for yourself or your listener, then there would be no reality or urgency about your expression. But granted that you *do* want the listener to see, hear and feel with you this experience, it *is* the reality that gives the delivery its urgency. Do you wholeheartedly agree with this thought?

10.   Honestly now, how is it that almost everything else is more real to you than the very things that should be the most real? Maybe you are different from many of us, but somehow the truths of God's word are far from the living, throbbing, vital realities they ought to be and that we want them to be. Why is this? Could it be that we do not live in the right world? We live in a material, physical, fleshly world when the truths we preach are related to the world that is different than and above these pursuits. For "they that are after the flesh mind the things of the flesh; but they that are after the Spirit mind the things of the Spirit... But ye are not in the flesh..." Cf. Romans 8:5, 9. To sum it up, I believe you will agree with me that we simply do not "take time to be holy." It *does* take time to make these truths we preach a living, walking, breathing reality to our hearts. One more question.

11.   Are you willing to pay the price it will cost to develop habits that will make what you preach such a reality to you that it will be delivered with the urgency necessary to make it a reality to those who hear? Before you answer, let me say that the price is terrific. But it is no more than a dedicated actor pays, nor than men in much more "earthly" professions than the ministry pay. It will take time, energy, prayer, practice, disappointment, discouragement and embarrassment, but to be able to make live in all its reality just one truth of God for someone for whom it had never before lived will be more than recompense. Are you ready to give yourself to your preparation for an effective delivery? (Your answer written here is important, but its record on your conscience and in our Lord's great record book is the most important.)

Assignment Twenty-six

Read the discussion carefully and work out the exercises.

Here is how you can develop reality in your preaching. Know this:

You must see before you can make others see.
You must hear before you can make others hear.
You must taste before you can cause others to taste.
You must cry before others will cry with you.
You must laugh before others will laugh with you.

Note this sentence of familiar scripture:

"But while he was yet afar off, his father saw him, and was moved with compassion, and ran, and fell on his neck, and kissed him." Luke 15:20.

Is this verse *real* to you? What I mean is, does it come alive to your heart as you read it? How can you give it reality? Obviously this is possible only by thoroughly acquainting yourself with it until you can feel as the father felt, walk in the sandals of the boy as he approaches home. Only when these feelings are yours will you be able to transmit them to others. But there are some very definite principles we can use in lending reality to these words or any other words. Let us notice some of them:

a. Study the text phrase by phrase. If we did so we could break the verse up into the following phrases:

(1) "But while he was yet afar off,
(2) his father saw him,
(3) and was moved with compassion,
(4) and ran,
(5) and fell on his neck,
(6) and kissed (Gr. kissed him much) him."

Thus we have six separate pictures to paint upon the tablets of our hearts.

b. Make a direct appeal to the imagination of your listener. To do this they must "experience" what you say. Appeal will need to be made to their *seven* senses. Note:

(1) *Visual.* What they see in imagination. They can be made to see the whole circumstance of the text.

(2) *Auditory.* What they hear. Can they so enter with you into your description that they can "hear" the father speak to the boy and the boy to his father?

(3) *Gustatory.* What they taste. The meal of the prodigal son is not spoken of in this verse, but it is in later verses. Make the mouths water in your audience participation of the description of the meal.

(4) *Olfactory.* Has reference to smell. We remember the odors of any circumstance longer and more clearly than any of the other sense factors.

(5) *Tactual or Touch.* Alan H. Monroe in his *Principles and Types of Speech,* p. 420, has broken this section down into the following subdivisions:

(a) Texture or shape: Referring to "how rough or smooth, dry or wet, or shape, or slimy, or sticky a thing is."

(b) Pressure: This has reference primarily to the feelings of physical pressure, although emotional pressure could be described and experienced.

(c) Heat and cold: This is referred to elsewhere as "thermal" type of imagery. The relations of heat and cold. Have your audience actually involved in what you describe.

(6) *Muscle strain.* Sometime called "kinaesthetic" imagery. This can be made real if you are "aware" enough to put into words your feelings. Have you ever held onto something until although you did not want to let go your strength utterly failed you and you had to let go? What were the sensations in your fingers and arms at that moment of forced release?

(7) *Organic.* Has reference to internal sensations. Nausea would be an extreme of this. Hunger, dizziness and other sensations can all be described so vividly that audience participation is assured.

Let us name the seven senses just described. It will be of no real value to us until they are known by memory and we can describe or define them in our own minds. They were:

1. —————————————————————

2. —————————————————————

3. —————————————————————

4. —————————————————————

5. _____

    a. _____

    b. _____

    c. _____

6. _____

7. _____

How does this relate to our text? It should be obvious by now.

Assignment Twenty-seven

Let each student describe the circumstances of the text, Luke 15:20, with a definite, careful use of appeal to as many of the seven senses as possible. If you can bring them all into an imaginative description of the text, so much the better. Whatever you do, do it with the urgency and enthusiasm commensurate with the reality of the thought.

Let half of the class approach the text from the father's point of view and the other half from the son's viewpoint. *Become* (in imagination) the father. *Become* (in imagination) the son. Feel it. Experience it. Then tell it. These descriptions need not exceed five or six minutes in length and must be written out word for word and either read with real emphasis or given from memory following an outline.

Assignment Twenty-eight

If you want to try creating the reality of other texts before you proceed here are some that should be fruitful of development:

a) Luke 16:23. b) Luke 18:11. c) Acts 8:38. d) Acts 16:26. e) Romans 5:1–2. (Note here that a text does not have to relate to some physical event to have reality. "Justification" — "peace with God" — are very real conditions and need to be made so not only to the hearers, but first to us.)

Our purpose in this assignment, however, is to go onward in our preparation for the most effective delivery of the sermon. There is only *one* way that we can experience the reality of what we write or speak. We must first understand the principles used in describing reality. This we have just considered. Then, practice, practice and more practice. We are so prone to be dull and dead in our mode of delivery. Not for many reasons, but because of one reason. The message *is not real to you!* Somehow we do not see or feel how vitally important it is that the message throb with reality. I do hope somehow you have caught the tragic need here. I am going to print for you part of a message by James Earl Ladd. It is called "Ten Seconds After Death." I want you to create the reality of this sermon both for yourself and for the listeners. You will have to visualize an audience if you do not now preach for one. To do this you will need to "enter into" the circumstance of the sermon. By appealing to the seven senses you must use words that transport you and then your audience into the different phases of the message. We did this in our class. Here is part of the introduction with the reality developed by three of the students (David Parsons, Harry Stirtz and Junior Ball):

"Ten Seconds After Death"
Introduction

"Shortly before his death Thomas Alva Edison, in his big underground laboratory in East Orange, New Jersey, was performing a very definite and delicate experiment. He had his great machine so adjusted that even the rise in temperature of one or two degrees, or a fraction of a degree would change the reading of the instruments enough to spoil the particular experiment under way. He had spent thousands of dollars getting this experiment rigged up, and just at the most crucial moment of it he felt, on the back of his neck, a draft. The door opened and there stood a newspaper reporter with pad and pencil to get an interview. How that reporter got past the guards no one knows. He looked at the instrument. The temperature was rising, the instruments were flying on the panels. Thousands of dollars were going out of the window. Edison had to get rid of the fellow and get rid of him in a hurry.

The newspaper reporter smiled and said, "I have come, Sir, for an interview. What are you doing?"

Mr. Edisón said, "This is off the record. I'll tell you if you leave immediately. You see those jars and tubes and coils and the rheostats? I've got a machine through which I shall be able to talk with the dead."

1. *Creating the reality for one's self.*

In your imagination picture yourself sitting before the instrument panel of a maze of scientific equipment. Realize, as you sit there, eyes transfixed on the panel, that you are nearing the close of your productive life and that there is no time to waste if you are to finish these most important experiments with which you have spent so much time, energy and thousands of dollars of expense. Imagine yourself sitting, deeply contemplating this enormous expenditure of physical and material resources, the delicateness of the equipment and the manipulation of the experiment, so delicate that even the slightest change of temperature could ruin it, and the magnitude of the experiment's successful completion. With these thoughts in mind, see and feel the mixed feelings of anxiety, fear, expectation, hope and joy that whirl inside your brain. Feel and express the muscle tensions which transpire as your eyes scan the dials and gauges, checking temperatures, tensions and other information, and you realize that the "zero" hour is but moments away. You know that all entrances are guarded so that no one can enter your underground laboratory during the experiment and destroy it; but yet, as the experiment begins, you feel a draft on the back of your neck as the door behind you is opened. In horror and anxiety you scan the dials to see them jump and fly before your eyes. In your shock you realize that thousands of dollars and hours and hours of tedious labor are flying out of that door. You whirl in outrage to see who would dare interrupt you at this crucial time and you see a newspaper reporter with pad and pencil in hand standing before you.

Now place yourself in the position of the reporter. Think how you have planned and dreamed of such a moment, one which would surely mean notice and promotion for you, an interview with this great inventor during this great and secret experiment! See and feel yourself smile amiably in your partial innocence of your blunder, but mostly nerve and audacity, and ask blandly, "What are you doing?"

Again imagine yourself in the place of Edison as your mind whirls for the answer to "How can I get rid of this bungling, nervy nuisance before he completely ruins this experiment?" And then you think, "If I told him some fantastic and supposedly secretive story, he would be out of here like a shot to spread the news."

Feel your reactions within as you calmly and with a "blasé" attitude say, "See these instruments, these jars, tubes, wires, coils and rheostats? With this apparatus I am going to talk with the dead!"

2. *Creating the Reality of the Sermon for One's Hearers.*

In imagination think of Thomas Edison, picture him in your mind and then think of the great things that he did. Picture him as he is going down the ramp into his underground laboratory, as he opens the door, and as he enters into the room and seats himself at the chair which is placed before the control panel of the precious machine on his left. Move your hand as if to touch one or two dials and then sit back and relax but regain quickly the tension just lost. Look strainingly at the dials until you are sure that they are in just the desired position and then begin to do the anticipated test. Picture the old man as he is about to start the test and go with him as his mind wanders back over the advance preparation, the building, the machine, the temperature control of the building, the men who worked faithfully so many hours, and the personal sacrifice of yourself. Feel with the excitement that comes when a great event is just about to take place. Then feel with him the sudden shock and the fear that runs through his mind as he feels that cold breeze running past his neck. Turn with him quickly and see before you the young cub reporter, dressed in his top coat, suit, and hat. Wonder with Edison just how he got past the guards. Look back at the instrument panel and notice the wild waving of most of the instruments on the board. Notice the heat gauge and see it as it starts to climb. Realize in your mind now just what all of this unnecessary change can cost; the countless effort of the many men who had worked for weeks, yes for months to put it in shape, the countless dollars put in machines and buildings. Feel the urgency as you realize that this fellow has to leave, and immediately or all is lost. Think of those sharp words which would cause the man to be thrown out and then discard them realizing that that would take too much time. Hear his words as he says, "I have come, Sir, for an interview. What are you doing?" Then relax a little as his words bring to your mind what you think is a sure fire idea for ridding yourself of this man. Speak up softly so as not to seem half serious. "This is off the record. I'll tell you if you leave immediately..."

Now become in imagination the newspaper reporter. Think of all of the glory that is yours if you can get this story from the man before you. Hear his words as he speaks of hearing from the dead. Think of all the great things that could be learned. Think of what this would mean to science. Relax a little and then in your hurry to get out, agree to what the scientist said.

3. *Reality Developed.*

With yourself as Thomas Edison get up in the morning. Your old bones are not quite as creaky as they usually are. Now you have your clothes on; you do not even bother to shave again. You go down stairs. You pick up the plate with the egg on it, gobble it down, and proceed outside to the old garage. The two policemen at the door greet you and open the door. You go inside of the garage and there another policeman unlocks the door leading to a large long stairway. You proceed down this to the heavy door at the bottom of the steps into the room which is well lighted from the many fluorescent lights hanging in strategic places. Your assistant greets you and you nod back and pick up the chart board. "This is the morning when we make the big test," you say to the man at the controls of the large black panel of a fabulous amount of odd looking dials. "Yes Sir," he answers back. You look at the dials on the board, then begin to take over the handles that raise and lower the temperature of the room. You send your man out of the laboratory and then begin to make things ready to start the operation. All of the time in the back of your mind hoping that nothing goes wrong to lower that temperature that will cause that chemical reaction. That is the reason why you sent the assistant out of the room. The tensions begin to rise in your muscles as you begin to make ready. Then the little temperature dial on the left starts moving slowly at first, then faster and finally it looks like a compass with a very strong magnet close by. Then the cool draft brushes the back of your neck and you realize that the door has come open. You spin around and see a reporter standing in that forbidden doorway, leaning against the door; a cocky reporter with his old felt hat on the back of his head with the brim turned up and the press card in the hand. He says to you in a pleasant, but a sure voice, "I have come, Sir, for an interview." As you look at the dials again you realize that if something is not done immediately the whole town of East Orange, New Jersey, may no longer be. Besides, you think of the money that would be lost, of the countless number of lives lost, including your own.

Now become the reporter as you are standing triumphantly in the doorway not realizing the danger that you are in and the danger that you are causing for others, sort of bragging a bit because you are here and have a chance that no one has had for a long time — an interview with Mr. Edison. Now hear those words as he tells you it is a machine for talking with the dead. After the shock passes, turn and run out the door, through the doors and on the outside and to the nearest phone and call your editor.

The purpose of this type of exercise is to develop in your mental make-up the desire and ability to give such reality to *every sermon.*

First the outline is made. But you have only the skeleton; will it be made to live? Preacher, will "these dry bones live?" Not by looking the outline over for a few minutes once or twice and thinking, hoping, praying that the reality of the thoughts expressed in outline will "come to you" on the spur of the moment. How much better it would be to write off a rough draft of the sermon as best you can from the outline and then rework and reword it, breathing reality and life into it by the means and methods we are here suggesting? If you really want to please God and reach the hearts of your congregation, can you afford to do less? Let me help you with the first phrase or two of the first division of this message and then you go on from there:

I. Ten Seconds after Death I Shall Have Entered a New and Better Life.

What happens to me ten seconds after I die? I believe, ladies and gentlemen, that ten seconds after I die I shall have crossed the threshold into a newer and better life.

Sub-proposition: Reasons for my faith in this new and better life after death.

Sub-division: 1. It is a reasonable conclusion.

Re-proof by analogy or comparison.

Years ago Dr. Alexis Carrel took some cells from the heart of a chicken. He put these cells into a glass jar. He invented a thermostat by which the temperature could be kept the same. He had a machine by which they pumped in beef broth and gelatin and fed that chicken's heart. He had a suction pump by which the by-products of metabolism of the cell tissue could be sucked off the top — the scum could be removed. For more than twenty years he kept that heart of the chicken alive in a glass jar.

I hope you can lead from this into the rebuke. It should not be difficult. But before you do you had better work out the reality of the above story. Here is how some of the students did it. First the statistics about Dr. Carrel to lend reality to the man:

"Carrel, Alexis, 1873–1944, American surgeon and experimental biologist, born near Lyons, France, M.D. University of Lyons, 1900. Coming to the United States in 1905, he joined the staff of Rockefeller Institute in 1906 and served as a member from 1912 to 1939. For his work in suturing blood vessels, in transfusions, and in transplantation of organs, he received the 1912 Nobel Prize in Physiology and Medicine. In the First World War he developed with Dakin a method of treating wounds by irrigation with a sodium hypochlorite solution. With Charles A. Lindbergh he invented an artificial, or mechanical, heart — a sterile glass chamber through which is pumped a fluid containing food materials and oxygen — by means of which he kept alive a number of different kinds of tissue and organs. He kept alive for 32 years bits of tissue from a chicken's heart. In 1939 he returned to France. He wrote *Man the Unknown* (1935) and, with Lindbergh, *The Culture of Organs* (1938)." *(The Columbia Encyclopedia*, p. 328.)

Dr. Alexis Carrel was a religious man and made these following statements concerning prayer in an article in *The Reader's Digest*, "Twentieth Anniversary Anthology," 1941, pp. 104–106:

"Prayer is a force as real as terrestrial gravity. As a physician, I have seen men, after all other therapy had failed, lifted out of disease and melancholy by the serene effort of prayer. It is the only power in the world that seems to overcome the so-called 'laws of nature'; the occasions on which prayer has dramatically done this have been termed 'miracles.' But a constant, quieter miracle takes place hourly in the hearts of men and women who have discovered that prayer supplies them with a steady flow of sustaining power in their daily lives.

"Today, as never before, prayer is a binding necessity in the lives of men and nations. The lack of emphasis on the religious sense has brought the world to the edge of destruction. Our deepest source of power and perfection has been left miserably undeveloped. Prayer, the basic exercise of the spirit, must be actively practiced in our private lives. The neglected soul of man must be made strong enough to assert itself once more. For if the power of prayer is again released and used in the lives of common men and women; if the spirit declares its aims clearly and boldly, there is yet hope that our prayers for a better world will be answered."

Then a description that gives gripping reality to the story. If you never used the more lengthy explanation of the story and spoke only the words as they appear above the line, what tremendous urgent reality would be in your words.

To picture this crossing the threshold into a better life, see a young man as he leaves the church after his wedding; see him as he drives to his new life in his new home; see him as he lifts his pretty wife up and carries her across the threshold; truly he is, at least to him it seems, crossing the threshold into a newer and better life.

See Dr. Carrel as he looks at the total heart of the chicken which is before him and then see him as he picks up his sharp knife and cuts off a good part of that heart and places it in the glass jar sitting on the table; the one with the thermostat for keeping the heat down or up, the one with the pump and the broth and gelatin, the one with the suction pump to remove the waste material. Watch that chicken heart as the years go by — one, two, three, four, five; it is still alive and still growing. How long can such a thing go on or can it go on indefinitely? Nineteen, twenty — it has been twenty years now since that heart was put into that jar.

But there is another section of the sermon. You see what you can do in giving reality to these words. It would be much better if this were your sermon and your words, but if you can do it with someone else's message I am sure you can do it with your own. Remember, appeal to the seven senses of yourself and your listener.

II. Ten Seconds after We Die Our Destiny Is Fixed.

Sub-proposition: Characteristics of our destinies after death.

Sub-division: 1. Of the lost.

Re-proof by testimony: What does He say? (The Lord) In the ninth chapter of Hebrews, twenty-seventh verse, He says, "It is appointed unto man once to die" — *once to die* — "and after this cometh judgment." One judgment for the deeds done in one life. Now go back to the case of Lazarus and the rich man. "Send Lazarus that he might dip the tip of his finger in water and cool my tongue." "We can't do it," Abraham said. "We can't go down there and you can't come up here because there is a great gulf fixed that none can cross." (Note that this discussion has naturally led into rebuke and has prepared for the exhortation.)

Work out in detail the reality of this section and read it with the urgency it demands. If you do not read it, give it from an outline.

SUGGESTED READING

Baxter, Batsell Barrett. *The Heart of the Yale Lectures.* p. 174–183.

Brown, Charles Reynolds. *The Art of Preaching.* p. 155–187.

Kirkpatrick, Robert White. *The Creative Delivery of Sermons.* p. 18–27.

Chapter 7

The Introduction and Conclusion of the Sermon

THE WAY OF THE CROSS

Confusion reigned on that rocky road that leads
    to Calvary;
And the angry voices rose and fell —
    Like storm tossed waves on Galilee.
No hatred now between Jew and Roman,
    For they see here eye to eye.
Their cruel hearts seek human blood —
    Their lips cry, crucify!

While there 'neath the cross that sin has made,
    Too heavy for man to bear
Wrestles alone, the Love of God
    With the power of death and despair.
No sign of fear on that sad sweet face,
    As He labors beneath the load,
But only the look of a broken heart
    As He travels the Calvary road.

We need no help to follow the path He went
    For a furrow deep and plain
Marks the course that He carried
    The cross that day for a world of sin and shame.
There on the right stand the faithful few
    They walked where the Saviour trod,
While there on the left the jeering mob
    Daring the wrath of God.

And so through the ages the dividing line stands,
    Just as clear today.
You are either in Christ or with the lost
    For there is no middle way.

—CHARLES DE WELT

THE INTRODUCTION AND CONCLUSION OF THE SERMON

The Introduction of the Sermon

If you know not how to start nor how to finish you know not yet as you ought to know.* "Your speech is not well organized unless you kindle a quick flame of spontaneous interest *in your first sentence.*" And your message is not well organized unless it has a very definite persuasive element in its conclusion. If you have not moved men to act upon what you have preached, you have not preached. Please remember that the persons listening to you never took this course in homiletics. If a sermon is not interesting they are not going to listen — regardless of how well organized or scriptural it might be. If they do not listen — and I mean with the inner ear Jesus spoke about — then why preach? It is not just a good plan to have the attention and interest of your congregation, *it is an imperative!* Do you believe this?

* *Public Speaking as Listeners Like It.* Richard C. Borden, p. 3.

Assignment Twenty-nine

Suppose you were going to list the essential elements of a good introduction, what would you include?

You have heard enough sermons to do this. Maybe you have preached a number of sermons and will do this from personal experience. List them in this order: (Do this before you proceed further. Check and discuss your answers in class.)

1. As to length.
2. As to purposes.
3. As to wording.
4. As to mood created.
5. As to variety.

6. As to forms.
7. As to relation to text.
8. As to relation to theme.
9. As to relation to the proposition.
10. As to need.

Here are the results from a number of books in the field of homiletics as they wrote on the essential elements of an introduction.

1. Not everyone mentioned a time limit, but the consensus of opinion was that a good introduction would not exceed five minutes in length. (This was calculated on a sermon not exceeding thirty or thirty-five minutes.)

2. General agreement in the two-fold purpose of an introduction:

(a) To attract attention to the subject and theme.
(b) To obtain lively interest in the theme.

3. We will have more to say about the wording of the introduction. Suffice it to say here that this is very, very important. This is your first impression upon the audience for this sermon and it should be a good one.

4. It is generally agreed that although attention and interest must be obtained, no introduction should begin on a high level of dynamic development since there is always the very real danger of promising more than you are able to deliver.

5. There are several remarkable features about doing research in the field of homiletics. Not the least among these is the striking similarity in the method of development of the various parts of the sermon. There are a number of authors ancient and modern who suggest a dozen or more types of introductions. Could you list three ways of introducing a subject? We will list several later in this lesson.

(a) ——————————————————————————————————

(b) ——————————————————————————————————

(c) ——————————————————————————————————

6. The introduction and the conclusion should have very definite form. This is unanimous expression of writers. Know

what you want to say in the introduction and just *how* to say it. A number suggested writing out the introduction word for word and at least memorizing a key sentence. To this let me add my hearty "Amen."

7. What is the relation of the introduction to the text? In some of the older books on homiletics an "explanation" of the text preceded the introduction. This would amount to an introduction of the text. This might sometimes be necessary, but we shall include it in the introduction proper. There is concerted opinion that the introduction should be a bridge between the text and the proposition. The introduction must not be "fastened on" to the text nor on to the proposition. There must be a natural development from the text to the proposition.

8. The relation of the introduction to the theme. Let us not burden people with our introductions. If you were to introduce a friend would you keep the friend standing before a stranger for ten minutes while you "circumnavigated" the obvious purpose of their presence before one another? So it is with an introduction. Its purpose is to introduce the audience to the theme and proposition. The introduction should be simple, interesting and plain, but never long. Let the audience "shake hands" with the theme as soon as at all possible.

9. The relation of the introduction to the proposition. From what has been said it would be easy to answer this question. It should be known by all that there are many homiletic teachers who do not follow the seven-fold development of a sermon. It is my persuasion that whether these seven parts of the sermon are delineated or not, they are still present. However, there is very definite agreement on the "aim of the sermon," i.e. the proposition. Having introduced the theme it will be then but a sentence to the proposition. In this sentence you narrow the scope of the theme to the one facet that is expressed in the proposition.

10. How will the introduction relate to the need of the congregation? Sometimes there is a special need. A tragedy has taken place in the community. A national crisis has arisen. Then of course your introduction can be worded and voiced in such a manner as to lead the minds of your people from where they are to where you want to take them. Under ordinary circum-

stances the congregation is not keenly aware of any particular need until you call it to their attention. Your introduction should set the general mood of your message.

Assignment Thirty

A discussion of the outstanding qualities of a good introduction. Exercises that call for your participation in this discussion.

1. *Simplicity.* "To begin a discourse in an affected or artificial manner is to insure its condemnation. Hence the introduction should be simple and unadorned... The simplicity of an introduction should be in expression, however, rather than in the thought presented." *Homiletics and Pastoral Theology,* Wilson T. Hougue, p. 104–105.

Here are three introductions which violate simplicity. Discover in what manner this is done and beware:

Text: John 1:14.

Theme: "The Great Condescension."

Introduction. Think of it. The Logos eternally with the eternal one, not only one in thought, but one in substance and purpose.

He condescended to clothe Himself, or rather to "empty Himself" of that prestige and power and dwell among us. Not that time called Him, for He knew nothing of time. Not that the challenge of being the Master teacher beckoned, for He had holier motives. Why, then, did He who existing in the form of God count not the equality of God something to be held dear? Only eternity can tell. But our purpose in the message today is otherwise. Shall we note the condescension of the Word?

Text: John 3:16.

Theme: "The Love of God."

Introduction. Brethren, what a magnificent thought to contemplate! As high as heaven's gate, as wide as this world of sin, as deep as Satan's hell is the wonderful love of our wonderful Lord.

> "If we with ink the ocean filled
> And were the skies of parchment made,
> Were every stalk on earth a quill
> And every man a scribe by trade,

> To write the love of God above
> Would drain the ocean dry
> Nor could the scroll contain the whole
> Though stretched from sky to sky."

What greater thought could course through your mind than this one? The theme of our message today. Note then some characteristics of this love.

Text: Gal. 2:20.

Theme: "Christ, not me."

Introduction. When God placed man in the garden of Eden He gave him through the image of Himself the power of choice. Even as Moses was to say in later times: "I call heaven and earth to witness against you this day, that I have set before thee life and death, the blessing and the curse. Therefore choose life that thou mayest live, thou and thy seed" (Deut. 30:19). This privilege was abused in the days of Noah when every imagination of man's heart was evil continually (Gen. 6:5) and man chose to do evil and brought upon himself and his seed the curse. Once again in the desert of Midian man chose evil instead of good, death instead of life. But we now live in a new age. We have the price-less privilege of choosing new life in Christ. And not only so, but of actually having Christ to live in us which is life indeed. These remarks lead us to our theme and proposition.

Exercises: Answer these questions.

a. What was wrong with the first introduction? Specify and enumerate.

b. What was in error with the second introduction? Give details and instances of error.

c. What was wrong with the third one? Please note that there is a basically *different error* in each one. If you want to check your answers, turn to pages 138–141. Do not refer to my analysis until you have made your own.

2. *Pertinence.* Pertinency was surely violated in the violation of simplicity. However, an introduction may be very simple both in construction and expression and yet not be at all pertinent. Here are some examples. Point out the particular manner in which these introductions are not pertinent to the theme or text:

Text: Romans 5:1–5.

Theme: "The benefits of the Gospel."

Introduction. There are marvelous benefits in the gospel. But then we would expect to receive advantages, for our choice to a large measure is based upon this appeal. Man has always been a free moral agent, *free* in the sense that he has a capacity for choosing, which is found in none of the lower creatures, and *moral* in the sense that he is responsible. His choices are made in the light of reward or punishment. The nature of man created "a little lower than the angels," when we consider his sin would call forth the question "What is man that thou art mindful of him?" The gospel provides wonderful benefits for the man who chooses aright.

Text: Acts 16:30–31.

Theme: "Your Greatest Question."

Introduction. There are great questions to be asked and answered in life. If you are a young man the question of your life's work is of great import. Surely all young men of true sincerity wish to answer this question aright. Well, they should for all of life is before them. The question of choosing your life's partner is of highest import. The high and holy estimate of the Master in respect to this should move us to ponder long before we set our lives together "till death do us part." But neither of these can compare to the supreme import of this question of our text, "What must I do to be saved?"

In these two introductions pertinency was violated in two different manners. Will you analyze and point out where and how this is true? Turn to pages 138ff. for my analysis after you have made yours.

3. *Vitality.* By this we mean that the introduction like the rest of the message must be alive. The subdued eagerness with which you introduce the sermon must come through to the audience. Once again we must say that reality is the only road to urgency or vitality. We could add that feeling has a great deal to do with vitality. If you cannot feel, you are dead. If the introduction does not strike a cord of response in the audience, it is dead. Will you criticize this introduction?

Text: Hebrews 1:1–2.

Theme: "God's Last Word To Man."

Introduction. In all ages God has spoken to man. We would

expect Him to speak to us today. There are many who say they have heard God speak to them. We must not judge lest we be judged, but the last word of God to man as found in Hebrews 1:1–2 is through His Son. In diverse ways and at diverse times God spoke to the fathers through the prophets, but now in these days He has spoken unto us through His Son. The ordinary and yet important question is, "Will we hear His Son?" It is not the intention of this sermon to exhaust the subject, but to observe in a simple straightforward manner some of the points in God's last word to man.

Exercise: We have now read and evaluated six different introductions. From the text and theme of one of these, shall we now formulate an introduction that embodies the three essential elements of which we have spoken? Select one of the texts and themes and write out an introduction. Read it in class for an evaluation and criticism. We realize that the introduction we here prepare could be greatly altered if we were to develop the sermon suggested by the text and theme and find that the development did not match the introduction. But our purpose is served by our exercise, so proceed.

Assignment Thirty-one

> Read this discussion of the several types of introductions
> and fill out the various exercises included.

There are probably more than ten different ways of approaching a subject, the subject itself being a large determining factor, but we propose to suggest at least ten.

1. *An introduction from the context.* This could have reference to a few verses or a whole book. Suppose your text was John 17:20–23. In these verses we have our Lord's prayer for unity. In what better way could it be introduced than to explain the circumstances of that prayer as it appears in the earlier verses? Remember that even when introducing from the context it must needs be simple, pertinent and vital.

"Unconscious Influence," by Horace Bushnell.

Text: John 20:8, "Then went in also that other disciple."

Introduction: "In this slight touch or turn of history is opened to us, if we scan it closely, one of the most serious and fruitful chapters of Christian doctrine. Thus it is that men are ever touching unconsciously the springs of motion in each other; thus it is that one man without thought or intention or even a consciousness of the fact is ever leading some other after him. Little does Peter think, as he comes up where his doubting brother is looking into the sepulcher and goes straight in, after his peculiar manner, that he is drawing in his brother apostle after him. As little does John think when he loses his misgivings and goes into the sepulcher after Peter, that he is following his brother. And just so, unawares to himself, is every man the whole race through laying hold of his fellow-man to lead him where otherwise he would not go." As quoted by O. S. Davis in *Principles of Preaching*, p. 21.

2. *An introduction from the text.* There sometimes is no context to our text. At least it is not apparent to you. If we used the text of II Cor. 5:17 we would have the theme: "A New Creature." If you look up a very careful exegesis of these words and formed them into a vitally applicable explanation, it would serve as a splendid introduction to this subject.

"Behind and Before," by J. H. Jowett.

Text: Ps. 139:5, "Thou hast beset me behind and before, and laid Thine hand upon me."

Introduction: "Thou has beset me behind." He deals with the enemy in the rear, the foe that lurks in my yesterdays. He does not ignore the dark heritage that bears down upon me from the past. "And before!" He deals with the enemy in the front, the foe that seems to hide in my tomorrows. "And laid Thine hand upon me!" He deals with the immediate contingency and gives me a present consciousness of ample defense and security. *Ibid.* p. 211–212.

3. *Narrative type introduction.* This can be from the text if your text carries a narration. Suppose you chose a portion of the story of David and Goliath. The section you wish to emphasize could be told in a most effective manner. That is if you tell it in the first person as much as possible. *Do not* start out by saying, "You all know the story of David and Goliath..." If the story is old and dull and drab and dead, why tell it? Make it live anew. In imagination transfer yourself to that time and place. See, hear, feel the circumstances you are to describe.

All of the narrative need not be told in the first person. It can be introduced as a story of the Old Testament and then transferred to the first person. The narrative can sometimes be interrupted to inject some modern application or comment. It can be concluded in the second or third person. Remember that this narrative must be pertinent to your theme and truly serve as an introduction. It also must not exceed five or six minutes so you will have to know what you want to say and just how to say it.

"Christ among the Common Things of Life," by W. J. Dawson.

Text: John 21:9, 12, "As soon then as they were come to land they saw a fire of coals there, and fish laid thereon, and bread. Jesus saith unto them, Come and dine."

Introduction: "I cannot read these words without indulging for a moment in a reminiscence. Not long ago, in the early morning, while all the world slept, I stood beside the Sea of Tiberias, just as the morning mist lifted, and watched a single brown-sailed fishing boat making for the shore and the tired fishermen dragging their net to land. In that moment it seemed to me as if more than the morning mist lifted. Twenty centuries seemed to melt like the mist and the twenty-first chapter of John's gospel seemed to enact itself before my eyes. For so vivid was the sense of something familiar in the scene, so mystic was the hour, that I scarce would have been surprised had I seen a fire of coals burning on the shore and heard the voice of Jesus inviting these tired fishermen to come and dine." *Ibid.* p. 212–213.

A second type of narrative introduction is found in the skillful selection of a story or illustration which is not a part of the text, but serves to illustrate and introduce the theme.

If your text was Rev. 19:16, your theme was "King of Kings," you could introduce your theme with this story:

"How many of you brethren have ever heard of Tex Rickard? Who was he? Tell me, someone. A prize fight promoter. In his early days Tex Rickard ran a combination red-light house, saloon and gambling hall in Dawson City in the Klondike. One afternoon there occurred at his gambling house something that made a tremendous impression upon the people who heard it. I can use that illustration as the best springboard tonight for our subject "The King of Kings."

"It was sixty degrees below zero. The icy air had a bite like a driven nail. A gigantic man, dressed in a parka and mukluks (Eskimo clothing), came into the saloon and stepped over into the corner, pulled his parka off over his head, took off his mittens and kicked out of his mukluks.

"The bartender, crooking his finger at him said, 'Come over, stranger, it's on the house. Warm up.' He shoved a bottle of whiskey across the bar.

"The stranger shook his head and said, 'No, thank you, Sir. I do not choose to warm up that way.' Going into the corner farthest away from the stove he rubbed circulation back into his hands. He combed the icicles out of his beard and then, coming up closer and closer to the stove, he warmed his hands until his fingers worked just right. Then he went over to one of the gaming tables and picked up a deck of cards and cutting through them, he came to the King of Clubs. Holding it between his thumb and forefinger he stepped up on the bar and said, 'Gentlemen!' Immediately all the folks congregated and the girls from the dance hall beyond came dragging their escorts because they thought a new card shark had come to the Yukon with some tricks. He said, 'I have come to the Klondike to represent that King upon whose teaching every club and lodge and fraternity is founded.' He turned back to the deck and pulled a second king — the King of Diamonds. Raising his voice to a rich lilting tenor, he sang that song which we all know, 'My father is rich in houses and lands, He holdeth the wealth of the world in His hands; of rubies, of diamonds, of silver and of gold, His coffers are full. He has riches untold.' He said, 'I have come to the Klondike to represent that King, the gates of whose city are of solid pearl and the streets are paved with gold.'

"He turned back to the deck and pulled out the King of Spades. He said, 'Yesterday, mushing my way over the Dawson Trail, I saw some men in a creek bed with a great bonfire thawing out the dirt. Then with pickax and spade I watched them bury a loved one.' He said, 'I have come to the Klondike, Ladies and Gentlemen, to represent that King who, when He comes again, will undo the work of the spade and empty every grave.'

"He then took the last King, the King of Hearts. He took the four face cards and tore them in two. He took the eight pieces and threw them in the teeth of the crowd and said, 'I have come to the Klondike to represent the King of Kings, and the Lord of Lords, Jesus Christ, God's Son and your Saviour.'

"In a silence so thick you could cut it, he went over into the corner of the room, pulled his parka on over his head, stepped into his mukluks, pulled on his mittens and disappeared into the night. Men in the Northwest, who listened to what happened nearly fifty years ago, say they still dream about that incident. The most *powerful, driving, biting* sermon they ever heard on the King of Kings and Lord of Lords." (From *As Much As In Me Is* by James Earl Ladd, p. 33–34.)

This type of illustration is what some writers refer to as the "shock type" illustration and here would serve as the "shock type" introduction. This is good from time to time, but will not serve at all as a steady diet for it will lose its effectiveness by too often a repetition. Another word needs to be said and that is if you do not have something in your message to match and better the illustration for force and appeal, you had best not tell it.

4. *The thematic introduction.* Here the emphasis is upon the theme or topic of the sermon. The above illustration from Ladd is thematic in that the text is used only to suggest the theme. Here is another example in which the theme is the basis of the introduction.

Text: Rom. 5:1.

Theme: "Peace."

Introduction: "It will be a long time before the incident is forgotten when Neville Chamberlain, with care worn face but triumphant gesture, stepped from a plane which had brought him from an interview with Hitler at Munich. Waving a paper, he shouted to the people who had come to meet him: 'Peace in our time.' Alas, it was a short-lived peace for it was based upon the promise of an utterly untrustworthy person, to whom a solemn promise meant nothing. How different is the word of another Man who left His home in heaven to bring to a sin-stained and war torn earth a peace that is eternal..." (As quoted by Alfred P. Gibbs in *The Preacher and His Preaching,* p. 181–182.)

5. *The startling introduction:* This can be accomplished in a single sentence or statement such as I heard one preacher give: "I'm going to prove to you that Hitler was born in Washington,

D.C." That caused a real stir in the congregation, but it promised the absurd and impossible. What he did try to prove was the questionable thought that "Aryanism" originated in Washington, D.C. and that without this theory Hitler would have been powerless. What a let-down! But there *is* a legitimate and effective use of the startling statement. Many times an audience has slipped, for one reason or fourteen, into a lethargic attitude from which they must be awakened.

Suppose you were preaching on the responsibility of parents to children. Could you from our present juvenile problem create a shock sentence? Try it. Do not get too far off the beaten path in your statement or you will not get back.

6. *The problem introduction:* This is always a good way to arouse interest providing the problem is real, pertinent and one that relates to the lives of those who listen.

If your text was Jas. 1:13–15 and your theme was "Temptation," how could you introduce this subject as a problem to be solved? With a little imagination it would not be at all difficult to do this.

Suppose you started this theme by saying: "I heard a man once blame God for his sin, and in his heart he believed he had a case to present. What shall we say to this man? Have you ever felt like Adam of old when he replied in thought, 'But God, the woman thou *gavest* me did it'?"

If you had as a text I Cor. 16:1–2 and as a theme "Money," how would you formulate a "problem" introduction? Try it.

Write out an introduction of this text and theme: Rom. 12:1–2, "Holiness."

7. Andrew Blackwood calls this next type of introduction "A striking quotation" (*The Preparation of Sermons*, p. 117). The only caution is that it be a "striking" quotation. We do not mean sensational, although some persons might catalog what you select as such. The point we are making is that the quotation *must* relate to the subject, and that directly so.

The words of famous men in a field where you are sure everyone is acquainted with such persons would be first on the list of "striking quotations." There are several books in print containing quotations from famous men on almost any subject. Suppose you find a striking quotation to start out each of these sermons:

1. Text: John 19:14.
   Theme: "Behold Your King."
2. Text: John 15:13.
   Theme: "Greater Love."
3. Text: John 10:14.
   Theme: "The Good Shepherd."

You can use any source available, but after having found the quotation, learn it well enough so that you can strike interest and attention by your presentation as well as by your content.

8. *The current event introduction:* Here are three excerpts from the daily paper. Will, you please find a text and theme to fit them?

   a. *Five Die in Head-on Crash During Fog*

   Oxford, Pa., July 7 — Five persons were killed, including two young children, in a shattering head-on crash early Saturday on fog-shrouded U.S. Highway 1 near Oxford. State police made a tentative identification of the dead.

   b. *Boy Killed by Rope*

   Clearwater, Fla., July 7 — Albert Cervalo, Jr. was killed Friday when a rope which he had placed around his neck and dangled out the window of a moving truck became tangled in the rear wheels.

   c. *Boy Returns $150.00 Stolen at Drive-In*

   Abilene, Tex., July 14 — The $150 stolen from L. J. Black, owner of the Dairy Delight Drive-In Thursday night was returned Friday by the thief, a 14-year old boy. The boy returned the money about 8 p.m. Friday. He told police he went in the drive-in, saw the sack in the open drawer, took the money and left. Black said he was willing to forget the matter.

9. *The direct statement type of introduction:* This is perhaps the shortest of all types of introductions. A generic statement of purpose is to be given first then the transition to the specific point leading to the theme and the proposition. Let us think out well the wording of the direct approach. Make it forceful and appealing.

If your text were: Matt. 11:28, the theme "The Wonderful Invitation," how would you formulate a direct statement that would intrigue the interest and stimulate a desire to hear?

Try the same procedure on the text of John 8:58 and the theme of "The Great I Am."

10. *The indirect or hidden approach:* This can be a most interesting and helpful approach. Start in a way and manner that does not at all indicate where you are planning on leading the folk. This can be done in a great variety of ways. An illustration, a current event, or any of the above mentioned manners of introduction. You must, of course, have in your mind the exact plan and purpose of your effort. Try an indirect approach to this text and theme:

Rom. 6:1–4.

"The Greatest Sin of the Saints" (cf. vs. 1).

The Conclusion of the Sermon

Of all the tragic neglects, it is the neglect of a well planned conclusion. Because too many preachers are lazy to begin with, they put off the preparation of the message until the last minute and if they do get up what they feel is a good sermon (which is open to question) they feel that the force of the message will make a good conclusion for the sermon. The thought must be that if it is a good sermon it will form its own conclusion. But if you have preached for any length of time, you know this is not true. But then, maybe some preachers do not feel that a sermon needs a formal conclusion — just a closing hymn and go home. Is that what you feel, brother? Why all the effort of preaching if we leave no call for action?

Why does the salesman present the points of his product? So he can close his book and go home? No. He wants a sale — some action. Why does a lawyer prepare his brief? Why plead the points of the case? A decision. If you are not preaching for a decision you are not preaching in the N.T. sense of the word. Paul, Peter, Stephen, Barnabas, preached for decisions. *It is in the conclusion of the sermon that you get the decision.* Brother, if you do not prepare the introduction, at least prepare the conclusion. If you have little or no development under some main divisions, *please* prepare the conclusion. If you have only three hours to prepare the message (heaven forbid) spend one hour on the conclusion. It is inexcusable and wicked not to leave a good — and I mean effective — conclusion to every sermon. Souls must be reached. It is here that you call for action. Do it!

First in a general way, what are the characteristics of an effective conclusion?

Assignment Thirty-two

From the following list, select what you feel are the three most essential characteristics of an effective conclusion, basing your selection on the conclusions you have heard or used. Write a paragraph on each characteristic. Do this before reading further. Read and criticize comments in class.

1. Brief as possible.
2. Climactic.
3. Pertinent.
4. "Wooing" or persuasive.
5. Varied.
6. Productive.
7. Well planned.

1. A good conclusion should be as brief as possible. We mean as brief as is necessary to accomplish its purpose. After all, if you have not led your audience to a place where they are ready to act, you will not be able to do it in conclusion. What gives you reason to think you could accomplish in five or six minutes what you could not accomplish in twenty or thirty? Even if you did succeed in stirring the audience to action by your conclusion, if such action is not based squarely on your proposition many, many times such responses are shallow and will not last. Usually five or six minutes will be ample time for a conclusion. You should lead naturally into the conclusion — not break in the sermon creating the impression "Now I'm through with my sermon, here comes my conclusion." Never, never do this.

2. A good conclusion will be the climax of the sermon. After all, is it not here that you expect responses? Oh, how my heart burns for the times when I stood in an audience at the close of a challenging, rebuking, wooing sermon and felt the pull of the truth of God. This can only be when you know the end from the beginning. All climaxes will not be alike. It will depend entirely on the type of appeal you are making, but all must call to Christ and the life that is in Him. There should be the force of the very Spirit of God in the conclusion of the sermon. Something of the sensation of standing in the awesome presence of the Almighty Himself. A call to the conscience and will that is well nigh impossible to deny. No "frazzling" out at the end of the sermon as

if "the lecture is now over, let us pick up our books and go home"; or, "I have now done my duty for another week as your preacher. We can now sing the closing song and we will all get about what we really want to do." Where is the Lord God of Elijah? Not only the fervent effectual prayer of a righteous man availeth much, but the fervent effectual conclusion of a righteous man availeth much in its working. When I say "fervent" I do not want to create the impression that always and forever we must manifest the *same* type or manner of fervency. No monotony is good and the same type of fervency can and will become monotonous; but more about that later.

3. A good conclusion is pertinent. I mean by this that it is based upon the proposition of your sermon. It does NOT conclude the last division of your sermon. Its appeal is broader and stronger than that. It is calling for action from the whole aim of the message — not from a part of it. Look back to chapter three (p. 49–65) and see again the picture of the whole sermon and the relationship of the conclusion to the whole sermon. There is some *one* thing (maybe sub-divided) that you want to ask your audience to do. What is the *application* of your whole sermon? Even a five cent pencil has a point. What is the point of your sermon? The audience should be asking, like Isaiah of old, "Lord, what wilt thou have me to do?" You know what your Lord wants them to do about the particular sermon you have just preached, and they do, too, if the sermon has been effective, and they do not ask for information so much as a *way* to act. This you must give them in the conclusion. But it cannot and must not be generic, but specific — the whole conclusion "woof and warp" formed with the proposition as the guiding factor. This will be clearer to you when we begin to work out some conclusions together.

4. A good conclusion must be "wooing" or persuasive. We have already touched on this before and have said about all we want to say upon it. Just one more word about that little word "wooing." I like the tenderness that word carries for me and that is exactly the essential element of a good conclusion. Compassion must ever be behind and above all appeals. Of course, it goes without saying that a conclusion should be appealing. But what is the quality of that appeal? Love, real genuine selfless love, must be the motive

for all persuasion. If you do not love your congregation they will know it. You cannot fake love and make it effective. O, you might try and no one will object. People will listen and maybe tell you what a "good" sermon you preached. "Good" for what? You cannot deceive the finer sense of the heart. If you have no true unselfish compassion for the souls of men themselves, they will know it. Perhaps they will not be able to express just what is missing in your spiritual life, but *they will not respond!* Some might "come down the aisle" in obedience to a "form" of religion, but they will have no more "power" than you have. Christ Himself must speak through you to the needs and lives of those who hear. They somehow must forget you and your manner of delivery and see the outstretched nail-pierced hands of the friend of sinners. This will never happen until self has been crucified *before each* sermon is delivered — until it is no longer you that live, but Christ living, wooing, calling, winning, through you. You may be dead and not know it, but sinners will. What will it be for you, oh builder, on the great day of eternal reckoning? Wood, hay and stubble? Or gold refined in the fires of self surrender?

5. A good conclusion will have variety. We should say that there are and should be many types of conclusions. All conclusions are based on their own proposition, but their type of appeal and development can be variously developed. There are at least eighteen different motives of appeal. Remember the list we gave you in chapter five under the matter of *exhort?* We are calling for action in the conclusion and the eighteen motive appeals used there can and do apply here with equal force. We plan on developing this thought in a later part of this chapter. Suffice it to say here that however effective a type of conclusion may be once or twice or thrice, repeat it again and its effectiveness is reduced in exact ratio to the number of times it is used consecutively.

6. A good conclusion will be productive of results. The conclusion is not the only part or even the most important part of the sermon in obtaining action. If you do not have something worth acting upon, you will have no response of eternal value. But after all, what is the criteria of an effective fisherman? It is not the tackle he acquires nor the stories he can tell, but the fish he catches. Are we not fishers of men? What constitutes a good soldier? Not his rank or uniform or what others tell you of him,

but the fact that he is "on service" and fighting a good fight. Soldiers of the cross, where are your service bars? And battle stars? How often have I finished a sermon and tried the best (?) I could and sinners resisted and refused and remained just outside the door of God's mercy. And then some good brother, hoping to encourage, will say, "Well, we never know how much good we do. The seed has been pl inted and it will produce a harvest in God's own good time." Somehow I have never gotten much comfort out of those words for they are only half true and are used too often as an excuse for second rate effort in preaching. "We never know how much good we do?" Well, we *can* know that several were *not* won to Christ. Can we rest in Zion while one perishes? Would you say the same thing if it was your son or daughter who was eternally lost? Surely we do "good," "eternal good" every time we preach the whole counsel of God, but that gives me no solace for those that I failed to persuade — like it or not, brother, if you do not get results in the salvation of souls, you have failed. By the way, when is "God's own good time for the salvation of lost men?" To ask that question is to answer it — God's time is today — *now!* If a salesman never sold his product and a farmer never harvested a crop and a carpenter never built a house and a clerk never served in a store, they would all be catalogued together as a reproach to their professions. But a preacher (?) can preach for weeks and months and sometimes years and have few, if any, responses when the potential was present for response, and what is said of this type of results? It is passed by lukewarm church members as "just the way it is in these days." When will we begin to admit to our own hearts that the criteria for success is souls won and lives changed?

7. A good conclusion is well planned. This thought has been most thoroughly discussed in the previous points — it is always better to practice than it is to theorize. Let us proceed to the actual development of a conclusion.

There are four steps in the development of a conclusion:
    A. Decide upon the basic appeal.
    B. Recapitulate the force of your main divisions in such a manner as to challenge and appeal.
    C. Recapitulate the force of the strongest "rebuke" element

in the message. Do this in such a way that it will call
and woo and win the hearers.
D. Appeal to and arouse the emotions on the basis of the
proposition and the appeal you have chosen.
Let us elaborate these points:
A. The basic appeal. For sake of clarity, we will reproduce
the eighteen basic appeals again.

1. Acquisition and saving.	10. Independence.
2. Adventure.	11. Loyalty.
3. Companionship.	12. Personal enjoyment.
4. Creating.	13. Power and authority.
5. Curiosity.	14. Pride.
6. Destruction.	15. Reverence.
7. Fear.	16. Revulsion.
8. Fighting.	17. Sex attraction.
9. Imitation.	18. Sympathy.

You most assuredly should refer again to chapter five if the
meaning and application of these terms is not clear in your heart
and mind. Look your sermon over very carefully and try to "feel"
just how it should end. By this we mean you should try to sense
what would be the truest basis for appeal through your sermon's
proposition as expressed in its development. Now you can take
the thought of your proposition and use one of the eighteen
motive appeals suggested here. Let me show you what I mean:
If your proposition was: "Characteristics of Christ's Church"
and your development was after this order:
I. A personally possessed church.
II. A uniquely individual church.
III. A church founded by inspired human agents.
How does your message relate to the audience? It should be
obvious that you are concerned with getting folk into the Lord's
body or His church. This appeal will run throughout the sermon,
but in the conclusion you will come to the climactic call for action. Upon what basis will you give the call? Look over the list.
Will you use:
1. *Saving?* The salvation of the soul that is provided in membership in His church.
2. *Adventure?* The real wonder and thrill that comes with

this experience of membership in His body. The marvelous new life there is to live in Christ.

3. *Companionship?* The relationship to the head of the church. The real privilege to work and walk with Him.

4. *Creating?* What you will be able to do as a member of Christ's church. The eternal contribution you can make to society and the world in so many, many ways; none of which you can make of any eternal value outside of Christ.

We could go on through the list, but you will have to do that in deciding upon the "slant" you want to give to your appeal. Remember now that whatever choice you make you have already preached your sermon and it is upon what is present in the minds of the congregation that you are building your appeal or conclusion.

What is the next step?

      B. Recapitulate the force of your main divisions with appeal and slant.

If you selected the first motive appeal "Saving," you then would or could say something like this:

"The church of the Lord was bought personally by the blood drawn from Immanuel's veins. But to what purpose? Had He not just as well stayed in heaven on an equality with the Father? It was for the purpose of saving your immortal spirit that He left heaven. Will His purpose be fulfilled in you?"

Note in this statement how the main division was reviewed, but with a definite appeal based upon the motive selected.

For the second main division:

"There will be but one flock and one shepherd on that eternal day of reckoning. He *is* coming again for His own. The question is 'Are you His own?' How eternally important it is that our souls belong to Him in a very real and personal way."

For the third main heading:

"The church of the Lord was and is a heaven inspired institution. Why did Christ send the Holy Spirit to establish the church? To elevate society? It has surely done that. To give man a better philosophy of life? It has given this indeed. But the answer to this question is not found in these by-products of the real purpose. The first preachers were inspired to speak the church

into existence as a soul-saving institution. Has its great purpose
been fulfilled in your life?"

Please, please do not *warn* the audience that you are now going
to review your main divisions. No break should be noticed. There
must be a natural flow of thought from your message into this
first part of your conclusion. In brief: Select your motive appeal,
run the truths of your main divisions through this appeal in
the most pungent, pointed, tender manner possible.

   C. This the third point in our discussion of "how" to form
      a conclusion is in practice the second part of the actual
      conclusion: Recapitulate the force of the strongest
      "rebuke" in the message with the appeal or slant you
      have selected.

When we say the strongest rebuke of the message we do not
necessarily mean the sharpest rebuke. Often the strongest is the
softest in expression, but not, of course, in truth. Your thinking
on this part of the conclusion should run something like this:
"What was there in the message that touched hearts?" Ma; be
(and many times this is true) you knew ahead of the preaching
of the sermon what part of it would touch which heart. You
know the needs of those to whom you speak, hence you not only
prepare a message to help them, but you can, to some degree of
accuracy, predict their reaction to what you plan to say. On
the other hand, there might be someone present you did not
expect, but whom you know and you sense how certain parts of
the sermon will touch him. Now, I am not suggesting personal
preaching of the obnoxious sort that lets everyone know that you
only have one or two persons in mind when you make certain
remarks. But you can know truth and the lives of people and
you know how they will react to one another.

Then sometimes the unexpected happens. A portion of the
message fitted a need you could not at all foresee. All this discussion presupposes that you are constantly and keenly aware
of your audience as individuals and not just as a mass of people.
You speak with conviction God's message to *people,* individual
persons. You see them and their individuality as God sees them.
You feel *with* them and you talk *to* them, not *at* them.

Sustaining the motive of "saving," here is the way the second
part of the conclusion could be worked out:

Your development of the first division could have the following subdivisions:

I. A Personally Possessed Church.

Sub-proposition: Characteristics of this personally possessed church.

1. It was bought with the highest price; this is indicative of its value.

a. *Reprove:* This thought will likely need "reproving" in a manner intended to make it a vivid truth. Folks need to read the blood-stained price tag of the Lord's church.

b. *Rebuke:* To members of the church you could speak in the spiritual realm. There is a constant need for a deeper appreciation of the meaning of being bought with the precious price of the lamb of God. Perchance you could say something in this vein: "Has it ever occurred to you how many thousands of dollars your parents paid to bring you to maturity or to where you now are in life? Have you ever really said a sincere "thank you" to them? Can you count yourself a true son or daughter until you have? But your heavenly Father has a higher investment in your immortal spirit. The highest price in all the world — the agonizing death of His own Son. Do your words and thoughts say 'thank you' to your heavenly Father for the purchase of your eternal soul from everlasting destruction?"

Then for the rebuke of those outside of Christ: "To *whom* do you belong? Not *what* do you belong to. It might be that you belong to some of the finest social orders in the world; that you are a member of this club or that lodge, but really that is not the query. To *whom* do you belong? Do you belong to Christ or Satan? Let me say that you do belong to Jesus for He bought and paid for you with His own precious blood. But have you recognized His ownership? Christ's church is simply made up of those who have recognized what He did for them on Calvary. What a tragedy it is for someone to die and leave you a marvelous fortune and for you to die without that inheritance. You see, if you fail to recognize His ownership on this earth, you will have lost it."

I have written out these rebukes in full so you will be able to appreciate how the rebuke is picked up again in the conclusion. What is written out is only the partial development of one subdivision, but it will serve our point. Not all rebukes will be used in the conclusion, just those you feel fit the occasion or better, the people. Here it is:

1. The recapitulation of the rebuke element to the Christians: "Are you going to say 'thank you, Lord, for saving my soul?' You will do so by a whole-hearted rededication of yourself to Him."

2. The recapitulation of the rebuke element for those outside of Christ: "Can you say with the song writer, 'I belong to Jesus,' Jesus belongs to me, not for the years of time, but for eternity?"

There might be a number of such pointed, pungent, prayer-filled remarks. It will call to mind the truth lodged earlier which by this time will have done its transforming work, provided it is in a "good and honest heart." Now is the time to thrust in the sickle.

Or maybe you will only want to mention one or two and lay special stress upon them. Whatever you do, remember, please, to be tender and loving as the Saviour of men even when dealing with the most distasteful of sins.

Another thing to remember is that you *must* have variety of expression and arrangement. This is why it is so important to work carefully ahead of time on your conclusion. Do not use the same adjectives and adverbs to describe the rebuke. Do not use the same number of recapitulation rebukes in every conclusion. Vary not only the number, but the length and manner of statements. I realize I have said this twice or three times, but it needs to be said more often, judging by results.

       D. The last part of the conclusion. This is at once both the most important and the most difficult. *Appeal to and arouse the emotions on the basis of the appeal chosen.* End with a call for action!

What was the appeal selected? What is the proposition of the sermon? These two questions accurately answered prepare you for this development. It might be well to look again at the picture of the sermon outline of chapter three.

To what emotion will you address your remarks? This is decided by the type of message you have preached as well as the audience. The manner in which you appealed in your last message will bear upon this also. Here are a number of emotions to which you could appeal. These should be familiar to you by this time:

1. Sympathy.	5. Personal accomplishment.
2. Fear.	6. Reverence.
3. Loyalty.	7. Love.
4. Companionship.	8. Gratitude.

Speak to the heart. If you want to know *how* to appeal to the heart, I suggest that you look back to chapter five to the seven forms of verbal support. Any one of the seven forms can be made applicable to the emotions mentioned above. Your proposition and motive appeal are the channels for this address to the emotions. Will you do it by an analogy, by an illustration, either hypothetical or factual? By specific instance or statistics or personal testimony? Will you touch one of the heart strings of man? This is your responsibility. The best I can do is suggest and challenge you to follow through on this section.

Assignment Thirty-three

We have now completed the sermon from the text to the conclusion. It has already been suggested that your sermon should be written out for the most effective preparation. In this assignment it is my strong suggestion that you write out in full a whole message from the text to the last word of the conclusion. If not time enough to do so, prepare a complete outline and write out the conclusion. Turn your outline or sermon in to your teacher and he will criticize it with emphasis upon the conclusion.

Here is a sermon analysis chart that should be of real help in checking the various parts of a sermon. This material could be mimeographed by the teacher and a copy supplied to each student for each sermon.

SERMON ANALYSIS CHART

1. General Impression.
   A. Does the message "grip" you?
   B. Would it meet the needs of the persons where you preach or attend?
   C. What general improvements would you suggest?

2. The Sermon outline:
  A. Introduction: (Give the main headings of the introduction).
    1.
    2.
    3.
    What type of introduction was used?
  B. The Main Divisions and Sub-divisions:
    1. State the main divisions either in your own words or those of the speaker.
      I.
      II.
      III.
        a. Were they well worded? If not, suggest improvements.
        b. Did they develop the proposition? If not, show why not.
        c. Were they forcefully stated? If not, suggest improvements.
    2. State the subdivisions.
      I.
        1.
        2.
        3.
      II.
        1.
        2.
        3.
      III.
        1.
        2.
        3.
          a. Does each subdivision relate and develop its main division? If not, why not? How improved?
          b. Your estimate of the reprove element. Improvements?
          c. Your estimate of the rebuke element. Improvements?

      d. Your estimate of the exhort element. Improvements?

3. What of the title of the sermon?
      a. Is it appropriate to the sermon?
      b. Is it clear?
      c. Is it interesting? How could you improve it?

4. The text:
      a. How was it developed? Expository? Textual? Topical?
      b. Is there a better text for this sermon? If so, where?

5. The theme:
      a. Were you constantly conscious of the theme being developed?
      b. Was it vital?
      c. Are you a better person because you listened to the discussion of this theme? Suggest improvements.

6. The proposition:
      a. What principle or principles of discussion were used?
      b. Was it too awkwardly stated?
      c. Was it hidden so as to not be understood?
      d. How could you improve it?

7. The conclusion:
      a. Your estimate of the recapitulation of the main divisions.
      b. Your estimate of the recapitulation of the rebuke element.
      c. Were you stirred to action by this sermon? How could you improve this sermon?

8. Illustrations:
List the illustrations and give your impression of the best and the worst.

9. Wording and style:
      a. List the words that were mispronounced or misused (if written, misspelled).
      b. How could the vocabulary be improved?
      c. List the figures of speech used.

    d. What was the one outstanding trait of the speaker?

SUGGESTED READING

Brooks, Phillips. *Lectures on Preaching.* p. 255–281.

Blackwood, Andrew Watterson. *The Fine Art of Preaching.* p. 99–112 and p. 125–138.

Spurgeon, Charles H. *Lectures To My Students.* (Condensation by David Otis Fuller) p. 208–220.

Chapter 8

Wording and Illustrating
the Sermon

THE STARLESS CROWN

Wearied and worn with earthly care, I yielded to repose,
And soon before my raptured sight a glorious vision rose.
I thought, while slumbering on my couch in midnight's solemn
    gloom,
I heard an angel's silvery voice, and radiance filled my room.
A gentle touch awakened me, a gentle whisper said,
"Arise, O sleeper, follow me!" and through the air we fled;
We left the earth so far away that like a speck it seemed,
And heavenly glory, calm and pure, across our pathway streamed.

Still on we went; my soul was wrapped in silent ecstasy;
I wondered what the end would be, what next would meet my
    eye.
I knew not how we journeyed through the pathless fields of
    light,
When suddenly a change was wrought, and I was clothed in
    white.
We stood before a city's walls, most glorious to behold;
We passed through gates of glittering pearl, o'er streets of purest
    gold.
It needed not the sun by day, nor silver moon by night;
The glory of the Lord was there, the Lamb himself its light.

But fairer far than all beside, I saw my Saviour's face,
And as I gazed, He smiled on me with wondrous love and grace.
Slowly I bowed before His throne, o'erjoyed that I at last
Had gained the object of my hopes, that earth at length was past.

And then in solemn tones He said, "Where is the diadem
That ought to sparkle on thy brow, adorned with many a gem?
I know thou hast believed on me, and life, through me, is thine,
But where are all those radiant stars that in thy crown should
    shine?

"I did not mean that thou shouldst tread the way of life alone,
But that the clear and shining light which round thy footsteps
    shone

Should guide some other weary feet to my bright home of rest,
And thus in blessing those around, thou hadst thyself been blest."
The vision faded from my sight; the voice no longer spake;
A spell seemed brooding o'er my soul, which long I feared to break;
And when at last I gazed around, in morning's glimmering light,
My spirit fell, o'erwhelmed amid that vision's awful night.

I rose and wept with chastened joy that yet I dwelt below,
That yet another hour was mine, my faith by works to show.
That yet some sinner I might tell of Jesus' dying love,
And help to lead some weary soul to seek a home above.
And now while on the earth I stay, my motto this shall be,
"To live no longer to myself, but him who died for me."
And graven on my inmost soul this word of truth divine,
"They that turn many to the Lord bright as the stars shall shine."

Chapter 8

WORDING AND ILLUSTRATING
THE SERMON

Just a word as to the purpose of this chapter. As we started in the beginning of this study we intend all of this material to be intensely practical. At the same time it is recognized that the practical becomes dull and monotonous without the note of inspiration and challenge. It is our persuasion that if you have followed carefully the steps suggested in the previous seven chapters, you now formulate a reasonable and forceful sermon outline. Whether you can develop that outline into an effective sermon is a question you must answer.

At the risk of being misunderstood, we want to venture another definition for a sermon.

"A sermon is *words.*"

Words are the vehicles of thought. The problem is that no one need ride with you if he does not want to. Simply because a man sits before you in the pew is no evidence that he is traveling with you in thought. If he does not like your mode of mental transportation, he will not ride. If your "vehicle" is too old or shabby, he decides not to go. If it is the same in which he has ridden often before, until he can tell you every bolt and nut, or better, to keep the metaphor, every comma and semicolon, he will choose to remain and not go. If it is too new and startling he might draw back through fear of failure or embarrassment on the way. Do not forget that he can get off at any station enroute. All the while he sits before you (if he is a well trained deacon or elder) he might have the most benign of expressions on his face and you would think him with you although he has never left the station of his own interests. Truths are fine, but

147

they ride in words. Words are the most important of all parts of your sermon because your sermon *is* words.

Let me venture a few positive suggestions about words:

Assignment Thirty-four

You must know the basic rules of grammar.

It is strange but true that young men can graduate from High School having only the most vague notion of the correct use of the English language. Here are some of the more obvious mistakes made time after time in the Homiletics class:

    a. The use of "you and I."
    b. The use of "lay, lie, laid."
    c. The use of "they and them."
    d. The use of "had and have."
    e. The use of "their" with "everyone."

(For practice you might try formulating two correct sentences apiece for each of these words.)

We can all play "ostrich" if we want to and hide our head in the sand and refuse to do anything about our misspelled, mispronounced and misused words. If you want a real rational "excuse" for not studying grammar, come to me and I will supply you with one. (The ones I have not heard I have made up myself.) But you know and I know that correct grammar *does* make a difference and will continue to make an increasing difference in the effectiveness of our ministry. Please do not take offense at what is to follow. I know most of you who read this book are college students and that you have graduated from High School, but let me ask you the question I asked myself. "Did you learn your grammar?" Shall we cease blaming anyone but ourselves for any deficiency here?

For further work in this area, see the books recommended at the end of this chapter. There is a wonderfully sure way to correct use of words; practice, practice, and more practice and I mean written practice, not oral.

The following material is selected from a High School text (*Composition-Rhetoric,* by Geo. E. Merkley and Arthur C. Ferguson, pp. 86–89.) It is found under the general chapter heading

of "Misused Words." As a teacher of others you should be able
to immediately perform these exercises. If you can not, study
until you can. Your effectiveness as a preacher is involved.

*In the following sentences substitute correct words for those
in italics:*

1. Apples are *plenty* this year.
2. The vegetation was *luxurious*.
3. It all happened *inside of* a year.
4. I can't go *without* he takes my place.
5. He wore a hat of enormous *proportions*.
6. A terrible accident *transpired* yesterday.
7. He keeps up the *observation* of the old rites.
8. He *demeaned* himself by his unmanly conduct.
9. He took a *deathly* poison and turned *deadly* pale.
10. I do not know what *character* you have for accuracy.
11. There was a large *audience* at the ball game yesterday.
12. He is an important *factor* in the prosperity of the town.
13. The seniors may leave the room; the *balance* of the students will remain.
14. He *completes* the book with a chapter on the Spanish-American War.

*By the help of a dictionary discuss the words in each group
below, and construct sentences illustrating their use:*

1. Aggravate, provoke.
2. Allude, elude.
3. Accept, except.
4. Accord, grant, give.
5. Admire, like.
6. Accredit, credit.
7. Decimate, destroy.
8. Demean, degrade.
9. Defect, fault.
10. Apprehend, comprehend.
11. Defend, protect.
12. Discover, invent.
13. Fly, flee, flow.
14. Fix, repair, mend.
15. Hanged, hung.
16. Inaugurate, begin, commence.
17. Lease, hire.
18. Purpose, propose.
19. Prosecute, persecute.
20. Proscribe, prescribe.
21. Promise, assure.
22. Learn, teach.
23. Locate, settle.
24. Present, introduce.
25. Stop, stay.
26. Transpire, happen.
27. Subtle, subtile.
28. Ride, drive.
29. Avocation, vocation.
30. Couple, pair.

Insert the proper auxiliary (shall or will) in each blank in the following sentences:

1. —————— we go to-morrow?
2. I —————— be obliged to you.
3. —————— I bring you the book?
4. How —————— I send the package?
5. Do you think we —————— have rain?
6. I —————— be glad to hear from you.
7. We —————— not soon forget this day.
8. He says he —————— be glad to see you.
9. John thinks he —————— go to-morrow.
10. He says he —————— not be able to go.
11. We —————— be pleased to have you call.
12. We —————— have stormy weather to-morrow.
13. —————— you undertake to do this service for me?
14. We —————— have to go whether we like it or not.
15. I —————— be lost, nobody —————— come to my rescue.
16. He —————— repent of his folly when it is too late.
17. Do you think that I —————— be in time for the train?
18. I —————— be obliged to enter into a minute discussion of the structure and parts of this sentence.
19. Let the educated men consent to hold office and we —————— find that in a few years there —————— be a great change in politics.
20. If she hate me, then believe she —————— die ere I —————— grieve.

If you have had no trouble performing these exercises then you also have been helped by a review. If you have encountered difficulty then it was good to know where you need study.

Insert the proper auxiliary (would or should) in each blank in the following sentences:

1. He thought I —————— be hurt.
2. I —————— like to see the Rhine.
3. We —————— prefer to go by boat.
4. I —————— be sorry to miss the train.
5. I did not think he —————— notice us.
6. —————— you be sorry to leave school?
7. What —————— we do without friends?

8. I ———— like to have gone on Tuesday.
9. He said he ———— depend on your coming.
10. Do you think you ———— agree with him?

Assignment Thirty-five

Then there is the increase of words as well as the correct use of them. How is your vocabulary? Do you use the same words to express the same thought time after time? Here are thirty phrases and sentences that are usually over-worked in the church service. These are not hypothetical, they are actual. There are other and much better ways of expressing the thoughts these words convey. Will you reword these sentences and phrases so they carry more reality? It is not that these words are incorrect or inaccurate (with a few exceptions), but they have been worn out. They are dead through overwork. The truths they carry are tremendous and are worthy of so much better vehicles. Will you please supply them? Use approximately the same number of words in your rewording.

1) "We are worshiping the true and living God."

_____

2) "This is Christian America."

_____

3) "When we have completed our study..."

_____

4) "We should clear away falseness."

_____

5) "You should receive the Word of God."

_____

6) "What shall we do to save our souls?"

_____

7) "Have you thought of your acceptance of Christ?"

8) "Christ is calling us."

9) "Undefiled by the world."

10) "There is a positive and a negative side."

11) "This is a fundamental concept of our religion."

12) "Man strives to that which is higher and nobler."

13) "The figment of imagination."

14) "God has always directed the worship of man."

15) "A great cloud over Mt. Sinai."

16) "They must give complete obedience."

17) "Jesus spoke as no man spoke."

18) "He spontaneously replied..."

19) "The revelation of God from on high."

---

20) "The book divine, inspired by God."

---

21) "The hope of the world."

---

22) "The eternal place of abode."

---

23) "The power of the Holy Spirit."

---

24) "The redeemed of all ages."

---

25) "Christ died on the cross for you."

---

26) "You should have an interest in spiritual things."

---

27) "It all depends upon you."

---

28) "This is more or less the essential point."

---

29) "Try as you will..."

---

30) "There is no other way."

There is no easy road to word mastery. But, every minute you spend in learning how better to convey the truth is spent in learning the most valuable information in the world.

It should go without saying that however well worded your message might be, if it is not spoken from your heart to the hearts of those who hear, your labor is in vain.

It is not that we need to add so many more words to our vocabulary (although this must never be neglected), it is rather that we need to learn the best arrangement of the words we already know. This leads us to the next assignment.

Assignment Thirty-six

> Let us now become familiar with the figures of speech which are such a help to the power of expression:

1. *The Parable:* The parables of Jesus should be sufficient authoritative examples of this forceful figure of speech. Can we not create parables of our own that will carry the truth to the heart? This is a form of teaching by comparison, of the known with the unknown. Cf. II Sam. 12:1-6; 14:1-24; I Kings 20:35-43, for Old Testament parables.

Suppose you invent a story or parable to illustrate the following truths:

    a. The lack of brotherly love.

    b. The profit of Bible study.

    c. The wide damage of gossip.

2. *The Metaphor and Simile:* Both the metaphor and *the simile* are figures of speech based upon likeness. The difference between the two can be seen in the statement of Jesus when referring to Herod. He said: "Go tell that fox" (Luke 13:32) which is a metaphor. Had He said: "Herod is like a fox," He would have used a simile. The words "like," "as," or "resemble" separate a simile from a metaphor.

How much more meaning and strength our messages would carry if we were constantly conscious of the meaning and use of these figures of speech. There are some rules for the best use of them. Metaphors are faulty when constructed in any of the following ways:

    a. When a figurative and literal statement are combined in one sentence about the same person, place, or thing. Note: "The Bible is a veritable mine of golden treasures. It contains sixty-six books."

The difficulty is that the mind cannot adjust itself from the figurative to the literal as rapidly as you call upon it here, and even if it did it would not find compatibility in the two statements.

b. When two contradictory comparisons are made in the same sentence, these are called mixed metaphors:

"His parents wished to pave his way over the stormy sea of temptation."

What is the matter with the above? We know the Bible speaks. of "paths in the sea" (Psa. 8:8), but not as stated above.

c. When there is not enough element of surprise the metaphor is weak. The whole point of the use of the metaphor is the shock it gives to the mind of the hearer.

When you say, "New York is the London of America" you have used two things of too similar a nature for comparison.

d. When the metaphor is carried too far, i.e. into too many comparisons, this can become ludicrous.

Just how long you will keep the metaphor before your audience is a matter of judgment you will settle by the immediate circumstance.

Please note that whatever makes a faulty metaphor will also make a faulty simile. Cf. Isa. 29:8; 55:10–11; 1:8–9; Lu. 7:32; Matt. 23:27 for examples of similes.

3. *The Allegory:* An allegory may be regarded as an extended or prolonged metaphor. This difference is to be observed. However, in the metaphor the real subject must be expressed, but the allegory requires that it shall be kept out of view and be indicated merely by figurative language. A good example of an allegory is found in Pilgrim's Progress. Cf. Eccl. 12:2–6; Matt. 9:16–17; Eph. 6:11–17.

Exercises:

a. Identify the following as metaphors and similes:

    1) "Ephraim is a half-baked cake."

    2) "Israel is a luxuriant vine, that putteth forth his fruit. . ."

    3) "James and John, pillars of the church."

    4) "The kingdom of heaven is like unto ten virgins."

    5) "I am the true vine."

    6) "The kingdom of heaven is like unto a net cast into the sea."

7) "Destroy this temple and I will build it again in three days."

8) "Their throat is an open sepulchre; with their tongues they have used deceit; the poison of asps is under their lips..."

9) "Keep me as the apple of thy eye."

10) "As the door turneth upon its hinges, so doth the sluggard turn upon his bed."

b. Form one metaphor and one simile for the following:
1) The way to heaven
2) The power of the gospel
3) The strength that comes through prayer
4) The folly of a lie
5) The need for study

c. Read Psalms 80:8–15 and Isaiah 5:1–7 for beautiful examples of Biblical allegories. Can you form an allegory on God's love for man?

d. Resolve in your heart that you *will* learn the use of these figures.

4. *Personification and Apostrophe:* It is because of close similarity that we state these two figures together. In personification human attributes are given to inanimate objects. Examples are:
"Wisdom cries in the streets."
"The morning stars sang together."
Not only is personification given to inanimate and abstract objects but human traits are often given to animals.

An apostrophe is direct address to an inanimate object as if it were a person. Direct address to that which is dead or absent as if it were present is also an apostrophe. This figure gives life to the inanimate in the same way that personification does, but the element of direct address marks the difference. See Isa. 14:12–20 for an example.

5. *Metonymy and Synecdoche:* D. R. Dungan has a most excellent development of these figures of speech in his book *Hermeneutics*, pp. 270–314. We give here some excerpts from his work: "Metonymy. — The etymology of the word indicates its meaning. It is from the Greek words *meta*, change, and *onoma*, name, hence a change of name; the employment of one name or word for another. Webster says of this figure:

"A trope in which one word is put for another; a change of names which have some relation for each other, as when we say a man keeps a good table, instead of good provisions; we read Virgil — that is, his poems or writings; and the 'have Moses and the prophets' — that is, their books or writings; a man has a clear head — that is, an understanding or intellect; a warm heart — that is, affections."

"Many times this figure bears a close resemblance to the metaphor and the allegory. All figures of speech are related to each other in that they are employed for the purpose of comparing one thing with another. The metonym is one of the most definite of tropes (figures). It is capable of such divisions and subdivisions as will enable us to apply definite rules in the exegesis of the passage containing it."

It is not our purpose to give an extended development of this figure of speech in the Bible. It is sufficient to know what it means and that it was used in the text. Here are some examples:

1. "*Metonymy of the cause,* in which the cause is stated for the effect.

"But ye did not so learn Christ"; i.e. ye did not so learn the teachings of Christ.

"Which veil is done away in Christ." Here the word Christ stands for the New Covenant of which He is the author.

"The letter killeth, but the Spirit giveth life"; the word Spirit is here employed for the New Institution which had been given by His inspiration."

2. "*Metonymy of the effect,* in which the effect is put for the cause.

"Cast thy bread upon the waters: for thou shalt find it after many days."

"See I have set before thee this day life and good, and death and evil."

3. "*Metonymy of Subject,* in which the subject is announced while some property of the subject is referred to; these things are meant, but the subject is named.

"Thou shalt love the Lord thy God with all thy heart." This means affections. In Acts 4:32, it is said that the disciples were of one heart and one soul — that is, they were one in feeling, wish, faith, desire to glorify the Lord."

"*Synecdoche* — This word is from the Greek meaning to

receive jointly. But the meaning now given to the trope is not easily traced from the origin of the word. It is usually spoken of as a figure of speech by which we speak of the whole by a part, or a part by using a term denoting the whole." (*Ibid.*)

Here are some examples of Synecdoche:

"For we have found this man a pestilent fellow, and a mover of insurrections among all the Jews throughout the world." Throughout the world is too large a figure unless we understand it to be a figure of speech.

Rom. 1:8. The faith of the brethren was spoken of throughout the world.

"The kingdom of heaven is like a grain of mustard seed." It would be folly to undertake to find an analogy between the kingdom of Christ as a whole, and a grain of mustard.

It would be well to check the sermons we have already written or a written sermon of someone else (the *Sermon Classic Series* would be a good source) and list all the figures of speech used. It might be that there is a great poverty of figures in your sermons. This is a sad lack. We have used examples from the Scriptures to let you observe that the divine writers used these figures over and over. Someone counted 164 metaphors in the first three gospels. If the Holy Spirit thought it expedient to so reveal the eternal truth to the human mind, "go thou and do likewise." But like all other good habits, it is only developed by practice.

There is a strong possibility that many who read these lines have studied these figures of speech before, but never saw any practical application of them to the high task of preaching the Word. Are you going to go away again and forget? Are we not way below the level we should be in our expressive powers? Can not this portion of our study be a real opportunity for us? Let us approach the subject in this optimistic light. All of these figures of speech will be used in the development of the "reprove, rebuke and exhort" elements of the sermon. What a marvelous appealing and convincing sermon we could prepare and preach if we only would. Will you take time and thought to do so? Souls and all heaven are waiting to see.

4. *The memorizing of scripture will enhance the wording of your message like no other one thing.*

But how shall we set about memorizing scripture? Let me say

first of all, *anyone who wants to can memorize* the Word of God. This statement is based on experience. Any part of God's book committed to memory is good, and all can memorize some part of the Bible. If you cannot memorize five verses, memorize one verse. If you cannot memorize one verse, commit a part of it to memory. What some people mean by saying "I *can't* memorize" is *"I do not want to memorize."* Let me say in the kindest way I know how that as a preacher of the gospel you ought to want to memorize His Word. There are multiplied blessings in this holy task. It adds to your knowledge, it fortifies your heart against sin. But it is not my purpose to defend this practice, but to teach it. Here are some suggestions I have found of great help in memorization:

a. *Determine that you will never memorize a passage for the purpose of exhibiting your ability.* When a scripture is quoted with any type of artificiality it is a sin against God. There are two extremes in this. One is the under-emphasis of the meaning. In this type of quotation there are just so many words one following fast on the heels of another; like soldiers in single file, they pass in review until the last one has filed by. Or worse, the artificiality is in the emphasis in which the meaning cannot be discerned for listening to the speaker. There are many who have a "preacher's tone" of one kind or another. The voice is raised and lowered as regularly as the tide of the sea. This some-what humorous poem might be in order here:

Now fades yon pulpit like a glimmering landscape
    on my sight,
And all the air a solemn stillness holds,
Save that the beetle-headed preacher wheels his
    droning flight,
And the sermon's drowsy tinklings lull the sleepy
    fold.

(With apologies to Gray's elegy, from *The English of the Pulpit* by Lewis H. Chrisman, p. 117.)

You should quote the scripture in the most natural manner possible, with all the change of emphasis the meaning of the passage dictates. You are not giving out with some "magical in-cantation." This is a word to the needs and daily lives of men and women; quote it as if you were the author of the words.

b. *Make an outline of the passage and memorize the outline.* This should be done before you attempt to memorize any portion of the passage. This outline should be as brief as possible, but it must be a direct development of the text. Write or type this outline on a 3 x 5 card and commit it to memory. (As to how that is done we will discuss later.)

c. *Read the passage to be memorized audibly twenty-five times.* It is my experience that no more than fifteen or twenty verses should be attempted as a section for memory at any one time. In reading audibly there is one very important factor to remember. You should read with emphasis. Transport yourself back to the persons who first read or heard these words. This will, of course, make it necessary for you to read for each passage the background material available. If you read the passage without the proper emphasis you will tend to quote without it.

d. *Commit to memory one verse or thought at a time.* This is the procedure to follow in doing this. Look at the verse and read it to yourself silently. Then read it audibly as if reading it to the audience; even visualize particular persons to whom this would have particular application. Now close your eyes and try saying the verse from memory. I do not have a "photographic mind." I know very few, if anyone, who have, but it helps me if I can think of a blackboard with this verse written upon it. To do this it will be necessary for you to write it out. If you can do it on a blackboard, so much the better. Proceed one verse or thought at a time through the text to be memorized. One additional thought could be added. If you will precede this exercise with prayer and memorize the verses while on your knees you will create more of the reality of God speaking to you through His word, which indeed He is.

There is hardly any real reason why any young man starting out in the ministry could not commit the entire New Testament to memory in a few years. To retain what you have memorized you must review it from time to time. However, it is true that after you have reviewed some passages enough you will never forget them. I know whereof I speak.

Exercises:

a. Prepare a brief outline of Acts 4:1-12 and commit it to memory.

b. Prepare for the memorization of this passage by reading background material. I will not list any of the many sources to which you can refer. I trust they are available to you.

c. Read this passage audibly with the feeling and emphasis twenty-five times. This could be done at one time or in several sessions.

d. Begin with verse one; read it silently; then audibly as to an audience. Close your eyes and visualize it. Quote it audibly. Open your eyes and quote it with feeling. If you cannot quote it or visualize it, refer to it until you can.

e. Do this with each of the verses. After having proceeded through several verses, you might need to recall the outline to prompt you in the relationship of the verses.

f. Do the same thing with Romans 8:1–11 and Philippians 2:1–11. After the exercises are completed at home the verses should be quoted in class, dividing them among the class so as not to have the same passage quoted successively.

Illustrating the Sermon

In this section as in all preceding ones we will not attempt to be exhaustive. To accommodate the words of Peter, "we speak (write) only the things which we have seen and heard." There are scores of books on homiletics and in almost every volume there is a chapter on sermon illustration. I would encourage you to read everything available on the subject (See the bibliography). What we wish to say here relates to your immediate use of sermon illustration. To carry out this purpose we will suggest certain types of illustrations in their order of importance and give a few words as to their proper use.

1. *Illustrations from the Bible.*

This is the first and the best source for illustrative material. To those who are just becoming acquainted with the Bible, or for those who need a stimulation of memory, a Biblical topical text book would be an aid. This particular type of illustration is almost a hobby of mine. There are some things in this best of all illustrations to avoid like the plague. One is *any* introduction to the illustration. All such expressions as "now let me illustrate the point" or "there is a story in the Bible" or "you all know the story" or "you know the story" should be left out.

The last two in this group ought to be cut out of our vocabulary and cast into oblivion never to be remembered again. What a reproach upon the intelligence of your audience to tell them they know what you are going to say and then to tell it in such a manner that they are sorry you ever mentioned it.

Simply to be acquainted with a Biblical incident that would illustrate your point is no guarantee that it will help your message. Indeed, if told in the wrong manner, it will do more harm than good. It is not that the Word of God will ever do anything but bless, but the uses to which it is put do a great deal of harm.

For sake of example, suppose you wished to use the story of David and Goliath to illustrate a point. First what is the *exact point* to be illustrated? Is it the thought of "courage"? If so, under what conditions? Are the conditions similar enough to the story of David and Goliath to make this Biblical story applicable? Is it "wisdom"? Is it "strength"? Is it "faith"? Know the *precise* point to be illustrated. Then read the story of David and Goliath carefully. Do not depend on your memory, however often you have read it before. Read it again before you attempt to use it as an illustration. As you read the story, keep the particular point you wish to illustrate in mind. Indeed, funnel the whole story through this aperture. If you find the story will not go through your "funnel," do not throw away the funnel and use the story, look for another story.

For sake of emphasis we will suppose that the story is applicable. You see here and there and in many places an illumination for your thought. The next step is to recreate the circumstances of the particular part of the story you want to use. Unless you have a longer time to preach than most of us you will not want to use the whole narrative. Prepare a brief introduction to the central incident you have chosen. Remember now that each illustration is complete in itself so it can and should be treated somewhat as a separate entity and not as a type of decorative appendage for the sermon. If you think I am exaggerating in the development and importance of the illustration, you might recall with me that all you can remember about many fine sermons is the illustrations that were used. If your illustrations cannot be remembered, it is almost certain the rest is forgotten.

The next step in the formation of the Biblical illustration

is to decide who is to be the leading character in your story. From which point of view are you going to tell this story? From the omniscient view? i.e. As if you were an onlooker who could behold the entire circumstances? This is the poorest approach in my estimation. You must not be detached or objective in telling an illustration. That is, if you want it to be alive to those who hear. Will you tell the story from David's viewpoint? Or possibly from the perspective of one of David's jealous brothers? You might tell it as the armour bearer of Goliath. When you have decided, introduce the viewpoint and then *become that person* and tell the story in the first person. It might not be possible to retain the first person narration throughout the story, but do so as much as at all possible. This can be overdone and it requires skill to know when you are close to affectation instead of actuality. Nothing is detected more rapidly by an audience than any type of pretense. Please remember that "the spirit of the prophet is subject to the prophet" and you should give the definite impression that it is with restraint that you say these things; however grippingly real the story may become, always let the audience feel that you could put much more into it if you chose.

Any type of illustration should be used sparingly. It is not necessary to give a narration in every sermon. When you use a Biblical story as an illustration, follow the above suggestions and make it live in the hearts of those who hear. The truth of the book will have to burn like fire in your bones before it will get some folk even lukewarm.

2. *The next best source for illustration is that of factual material such as biography, history, literature, and current events.*

Since nothing is quite so interesting as people, the illustrations you can find in biographies are probably the best. There is a splendid list of short biographies in Webb B. Garrison's book *The Preacher and His Audience*, pp. 137–138. In developing the material here you should approach it with the same type of reality recommended for scripture narration. Read this material until you can tell it with reality in your own words. Use the first person as much as possible.

Incidents from the lives of noted men can be most useful in illustration, for the desires and dreams of men have changed little in the history of man. The virtue and vices of men long gone from the contemporary scene are yet very contemporary in their examples for us. As in the Biblical illustration these men and women of history must live for you and in you before you can make them step out of the realm of the past for your listener. It is almost wicked to shut ourselves out from what we could know about so many people. Begin at once to investigate some short biographies of famous people for illustrative material. You will need to do some marking in or from these books so you can retain what you have read.

3. *Personal observations and experiences.*

We need to exercise care at this point. We are not suggesting that the preacher is to "preach himself." There is a certain frame of mind that the preacher would do well to develop. I refer to a type of sensitiveness of soul that makes him keenly aware of all that takes place about him. (The works of J. H. Jowett and Henry Drummond have helped me much in this.) When I say "aware" I mean to be able to look at all the animate and inanimate creation as God would see it. What do you see as you walk across an expanse of grass? Are you alive to all the lessons God wants to teach you? Is there a lesson in the patches of hard earth that shows through the lawn here and there? Can you see any more than a kind of fowl in the robin that stands with its head cocked listening? What word does that knarled tree, which was there before you were born and will be there after you are gone, speak to you? Does that cloud of dust drifting across the lawn from the wheels of a "hot rod" mean anything more than so much misplaced dirt? To ask these questions provokes some answers that you quite possibly had not contemplated before. When I say *personal observations* I mean the observations such questions and answers bring to mind.

Supposing Jesus shared your room with you and arose as you do to go with you in your daily routine of the preparations of the morning. If He sat opposite you at breakfast and followed you through the day, just what reaction would He have to those things that face you each day? If He would ask you to write down His observations, what would you write? Would He see any more significance in your daily round than you do? How would His holy, sensitive soul respond to what we so often hear, see, and feel? In a very real sense He *does* live not with us, but in us. It is the consciousness of His presence that makes us able to see "sermons in books" and stones, and in all of the very ordinary tasks and activities of the day. This so-called "homiletic mind" is a very delicate plant that only grows well in the warm climate of private devotion; and I mean prayer, study, and scripture memorization.

Our personal experiences are of no value unless they very definitely illustrate the very point we have to present. So many times we have had some experience that relates only in a general manner to what truth we are teaching. Avoid it. Do not tell it. In using any personal experience, please play yourself down, not up. The truth is to be seen, not the preacher. If it is possible to tell an experience without revealing your identity, do it. Most of all I would say let Christ be seen first, last and always.

There is a wide field to be explored in the use of current events as a means of illustration, but since my comment on this would be only second hand, we do not choose to develop this area. Dawson C. Bryan has a section on this in his book *The Art of Illustrating Sermons,* pp. 100–102.

Assignment Thirty-seven

Here is a truth for which you are seeking an illustration:

God is willing to save man.

We will suppose that you are illustrating in the area of exhortation.

a. Find two scriptural illustrations. Write them out, learn them and give them before the class.

b. Obtain an illustration from literature, either biographical or otherwise. Prepare an outline or brief of it and present it.

c. Prepare an illustration from personal observation or experience. "Let us provoke one another to love and good works."

SUGGESTED READING

Bryan, Dawson C. *The Art of Illustrating Sermons.* pp. 15–50.
Gilmartin, John G. *Increase your Vocabulary.* pp. 1–10.
Monroe, Alan H. *Principles and Types of Speech.* pp. 358–368.
Ramey, A. R. *Art and Principles of Writing.* pp. 43–72.

FOR YOUR FURTHER READING

Baxter, Batsell Barrett. *The Heart of the Yale Lectures.* New York: The Macmillan Co., 1947

Black, James. *The Mystery of Preaching.* New York: Fleming H. Revell Co., 1935

Blackwood, Andrew Watterson. *The Preparation of Sermons.* New York: Abingdon Cokesbury Press, 1948

————. *Biographical Preaching for Today.* New York: Abingdon Press, 1954

Blaikie, William Gorden. *For the Work of the Ministry.* London.

Blocker, Simon. *The Secret of Pulpit Power.* Grand Rapids: Wm. B. Eerdmans Publishing Co., 1955

Bounds, E. M. *The Preacher and Prayer.* Grand Rapids: Wm. B. Eerdmans Publishing Co., 1953

Bowie, Walter Russell. *Preaching.* New York: Abingdon Press, 1954

Brooks, Phillips. *Lectures on Preaching.* Grand Rapids: Zondervan Publishing House, 1954

Brown, Charles Reynolds. *The Art of Preaching.* New York: The Macmillan Co., 1945

Bryan, Dawson C. *The Art of Illustrating Sermons.* New York: Abingdon Press, 1938

Christlieb, Theodor. *Homiletics: Lectures on Preaching.* Edinburgh: T and T Clark, 1897.

Dargan, Edwin Charles. *A History of Preaching.* Grand Rapids: Baker Book House, 1954

Fuller, David Otis. *C. H. Spurgeon's Lectures to My Students.* Grand Rapids: Zondervan Publishing House

Garrison, Webb B. *The Preacher and His Audience.* Westwood, N.J.: Fleming H. Revell Co., 1954

Garvie, Alfred Ernest. *A Guide to Preachers.* London: Hodder and Stoughton, 1906.

————. *The Christian Preacher.* New York: Charles Scribner's Sons, 1921

Gibbs, Alfred. *The Preacher and His Preaching.* Fort Dodge: Walterick Printing Co., 1951

Gibson, George Miles. *Planned Preaching.* Philadelphia: Westminster Press, 1954

Hogue, Wilson T. *Homiletics and Pastoral Theology.* Winona Lake: Free Methodist Publishing House, 1940

Hood, E. Paxton. *The Throne of Eloquence, Great Preachers, Ancient and Modern.* New York: Funk and Wagnalls, 1888.

Hoppin, James M. *Homiletics.* New York: Dodd, Mead and Co., 1881

Horne, Chas. Silvester. *The Romance of Preaching.* New York: Fleming H. Revell Co., 1914

Hoyt, Arthur S. *Vital Elements of Preaching.* New York: The Macmillan Co., 1914

————. *The Pulpit and American Life.* New York: The Macmillan Co., 1921

————. *The Work of Preaching.* New York: The Macmillan Co., 1925

Jefferson, Chas. Edward. *The Minister As Prophet.* New York: Thomas Y. Crowell and Co., 1905

Jeffrey, George Johnstone. *The Warrack Lectures.* New York: Charles Scribner's Sons, 1949

Jones, Bob Jr. *How To Improve Your Preaching.* New York: Fleming H. Revell Co., 1945

Jordan, G. Ray. *You Can Preach.* New York: Fleming H. Revell Co., 1951

Jowett, J. H. *The Preacher His Life and Work,* New York: Harper and Bros., 1954

Kennedy, Gerald. *His Word through Preaching.* New York: Harper and Bros., 1947

Kidder, Daniel P. *A Treatise on Homiletics.* New York: The Methodist Book Concern, 1892

Kirkpatrick, Robert White. *The Creative Delivery of Sermons.* New York: The Macmillan Co., 1947

Knott, H. H. *How To Prepare A Sermon.* Cincinnati: Standard Publishing Co.

Macartney, Clarence E. *Preaching Without Notes.* New York: Abingdon Cokesbury Press, 1946

Morgan, G. Campbell. *Preaching.* New York: Fleming H. Revell, 1937

Morris, Fredrick M. *Preach The Word of God.* New York: Morehouse Gorham Co., 1954

Pattison, Harwood T. *The Making of the Sermon*. Chicago: The American Baptist Publication Society, 1944

Phelps, Austin. *The Theory of Preaching*. New York: Charles Scribner's Sons, 1881

Sanders, Norred Tant Cogdill. *Preaching in the Twentieth Century*. Rosemead: Old Paths Book Club, 1955

Shedd, William G. T. *Homiletics and Pastoral Theology*. New York: Scribner, Armstrong and Co., 1877

Stidger, William L. *Preaching out of the Overflow*. Nashville: Cokesbury Press, 1929

Taylor, Wm. M. *The Ministry of the Word*. New York: Anson D. F. Randolfph and Co., 1876

Whitesell, Faris Daniel. *The Art of Biblical Preaching*. Grand Rapids: Zondervan Publishing House, 1950

Printed in the United States
81118LV00002B/364-387